THE DON'T SWEAT GUIDE
FOR PARENTS

THE DON'T SWEAT GUIDE
FOR PARENTS

Reduce Stress and
Enjoy Your Kids More

By the Editors of Don't Sweat Press
Foreword by Richard Carlson, Ph.D.,
author of the bestselling *Don't Sweat the Small Stuff*

New York

ISBN 0-7868-8718-4

FIRST EDITION

10 9 8 7 6 5 4 3 2 1

Contents

Foreword

Parenting is, perhaps, the most rewarding and joyful job a person can have during his or her lifetime. Unfortunately, it's also one of, if not the most difficult and potentially stressful jobs you will ever have.

But not to worry! The editors of Don't Sweat Press have done a beautiful job in providing simple, practical and wise strategies that can take some of the pressure off of us parents. Whether you are just starting your journey—you're expecting, or have little ones—you have a house full of teens, or even if your kids are out of the house, *The Don't Sweat Guide for Parents* will be of tremendous service to you.

The strategies were written to empower you and to give you more options and solutions. They remind you that there are things you can do to take some of the stress out of parenting. The strategies point to the fact that, while some stress is inevitable in parenting, the rest of it (or at least some of it) is often self-created. In other words, we use our thinking in ways that take us away from where we want to be. As we become aware of the fact that we are doing so, we open the door to a world of options. Peace of mind becomes possible and, from that more peaceful place, parenting becomes more manageable.

For me personally, being a parent is the most important part of my life. Even though it can be difficult, Kris and I try to make decisions and create an atmosphere that enables our family to enjoy each other and to enjoy life. As I read the strategies in this book, they reinforced to me those ideals. I found myself saying, If I would do that...my life as a parent would be easier. I intend to re-read this book several times and do my best to put the suggestions into practice. I encourage you to do the same. I think if we do, well all be better—and much happier—parents.

Thank you for the job you are doing as a parent and for your commitment to your children. I hope this book is of tremendous service to you.

Treasure the Gift of Parenting,
Richard Carlson
Pleasant Hill, CA, June 2001

THE DON'T SWEAT GUIDE
FOR PARENTS

1.

The Hardest Job
in the World

There's a new person living in your house—a demanding new person who, though pretty small, seems to take up the *whole* house. And in between doing the new baby's laundry, feeding him, and keeping him clean, you suddenly realize that you haven't made dinner, showered, returned any phone calls, or even visited the bathroom—sometimes for an entire day—but it can all wait. You are compelled to attend to your new baby's every need.

Welcome to the hardest job in the world: parenting. True, there's no paycheck at the end of the work week, and for the first couple of years, there's no real vacation time. But thankfully, the rewards of parenting are huge.

So how do you succeed in your new job as a parent? For some, parenting is an additional career, not a new one. How do you fit into your daily life all the things that need to get done when you have a new baby and, perhaps, a nine-to-five job? What do you do about the dishes piling up or the laundry overflowing? What, in short, is the secret to getting it all done?

The key is time management! Your new baby sets a difficult course of challenges and obstacles for you every day. Your job is to successfully overcome each and every one. Learning to manage your time "the baby way" will take time. But once it clicks and you learn to prioritize your responsibilities, like any job, you'll find it gets a lot easier.

As for the dishes? Let 'em sit. The laundry? Try sitting your new baby on top of a running dryer while you fold clothes.

Just remember the big benefit that goes with your new full-time position: the endless, unconditional love you'll get from your children. What could be better?

2.

The New Parent Shuffle

The New Parent Shuffle isn't difficult to learn, and the steps can be a useful resource for delegating important parenting responsibilities. When new parents feel the effects of sleep deprivation, feeding, changing, getting up for the baby at night, or even playing with the baby can be deemed a "responsibility." It's a given that both you and your spouse adore your child and would love to spend as much time with her as possible. But add in outside factors such as work, sleep or lack thereof, and having to cook, clean, and shop, and even the most attentive parent might want to stare at the television rather than playing peek-a-boo after a long day. A little delegating can change all that and lighten the load for the stressed-out new mom or dad.

After the first few weeks with a newborn have passed, chances are that you and your spouse know your strengths and weaknesses when it comes to taking care of the little one. But don't let each other's expertise in these skills delegate who is going to do them each time. It's important to shake it up a little. If you've sung "Hush Little

17

Baby" night after night for weeks, you're probably aching to stop. A good idea would be to let your spouse step in and take over—the last thing you want is to think of singing to the baby as a chore. Both of you should have the chance to learn how your baby likes to hear you sing, and to increase your ability to comfort your child this way.

It is also important to create some rules. For example, whoever must leave the house for the office in the morning does the last night feeding before going to bed, then sleeps through until morning and promises to "take over" once home from the office.

Say you're a stay-at-home parent who spends all day taking care of your baby's needs. When your spouse comes home from work and offers to take your child for a stroll through the neighborhood, don't object just because it's bath time and you want to stick to a schedule. You've been the caregiver all day. Now it's your spouse's turn to spend time with the child. Let them go on their outing—or if the bath just has to get done, let your spouse bathe the child, and then they can go for their walk. Enjoy your quiet time alone, and use the opportunity to "refuel."

It's usually difficult for the primary caregiver to give up some responsibility—whoever changes diapers all day long knows it can be done better or faster. But the ability to relinquish responsibility is one of the most important factors in a successful partnership. Letting your spouse tend to the baby, even though you know you could do it better or faster or quieter, gives your spouse the practice needed to succeed, and builds confidence while doing so.

3.

No Such Thing as Bad Kids

Do you have a "difficult" child? Does your daughter throw tantrums for no particular reason? Does your son refuse to eat? About 20 percent of children make their parents nuts with exasperating behavior. Having a such a child can leave you feeling exhausted, depressed, unsure about your skills as a parent, angry at your kids, and embarrassed by their behavior in front of others.

A study that was conducted years ago, rather than blaming parents for less-than-perfect kids, concluded that children are actually born with a set of "temperamental qualities." These can be found as early as a few months! They determine, to an extent, whether your baby will be "easy" or "difficult." Though your child's temperament is influenced by other factors, for the most part, it remains fairly consistent for life. Perhaps your child's refusal to eat is in part due to stubbornness—a trait that he will most likely carry throughout life.

No matter what your baby's temperament may be, stay away

from labeling it "good" or "bad." It's not your baby's fault, nor is it yours or your spouse's. It's just the way things are! You yourself were born with a certain temperament—perhaps you get anxious in some situations. Chances are that you were anxious as a baby, too. The way you expressed that anxiety as a toddler might have been an inability to sleep without a light on.

Become sensitive to your baby's temperament early on. You can then modify your approach to your child's behavior to anticipate and avoid conflicts before they occur. You'll be a lot more confident, a lot less frustrated, and you'll have a happier, more loving, and more satisfying relationship with your child!

4.

Mommy Knows Best...or Does She?

Who knows best when it comes to proper childhood development? Most of the time, it isn't Mommy or Daddy who knows what's best for the baby. We're not child experts by simple virtue of being parents. There's a lot that we don't know—and it isn't as if our newborns came with instruction manuals. For this reason, it's always best to check with the experts when an important parenting issue arises. A parent should never feel funny or stupid when consulting a parenting book or asking a friend or doctor for advice— admitting you don't know the best way to handle some of the things that concern your children is nothing to be ashamed about.

Countless studies and surveys have been conducted regarding nearly every aspect of parenting. The common finding among almost all of them was that parents are confused and not fully informed. Take the issue of spoiling infants, for instance. In a recent poll, 57 percent of parents of children aged zero to six and 62 percent of all adults incorrectly believed that a six-month-old can be spoiled. In addition, 44 percent of parents of young children incorrectly believed that picking up a three-month-old every time he or she cries will spoil the infant.

According to child development experts, this is flat-out wrong. Most unanimously agree that if you don't pick up babies when they are crying, you can build up their levels of stress and distress, which in turn can slow their learning. Responding to your children's needs is not spoiling—your children need your attention to develop their faith and trust in you.

Those same surveys found that many parents have a misunderstanding of what can be developmentally expected of children. Another key finding was that more than half of parents do not know the age at which young babies can sense and be affected by the moods of others. Why is this important? Because research has found that an overly anxious or depressed caregiver can have a damaging effect on a baby's development.

What this boils down to is that we all have a lot to learn about being parents—even if we already have children! Most parents are not sure what to do when it comes to making the important developmental decisions of raising their children. But again—this is nothing to be ashamed about. Luckily, there are experts, books, and family physicians that have the answers. So the next time you hit an impasse with your spouse over what's best for your child, stop debating over who knows better: Ask around, read up, or call your child's pediatrician!

5.

You've Changed
(and Not Just Diapers)

At some point after the baby is born, just about every new parent gets hit with a sharp jolt of reality: I'm a parent! I now have new responsibilities to live up to. For some of us, this little epiphany comes early, before we even leave the hospital. But for others, the jolt may not hit for a few days, weeks, or even months. Sooner or later, though, we all come to realize that our lives have changed forever. Recognize these common changes that most new parents go through early on, and remember that they're all perfectly normal.

Confusion: You're a new parent? Chances are that you're suddenly feeling confused. If there's one thing that sets the first few months of parenthood apart from the next few years, it's the confusing and often conflicting emotions you may feel. For instance, you may be feeling the virility, the power, and the pride at having created a new life. But on the other hand, you may also feel helpless when you can't satisfy your new baby's needs.

Love: You will also discover in yourself the capacity for a new and different kind of love. Sure, you love your spouse. But there's no comparing the all-consuming love you're suddenly feeling for your child with the love you have for anybody else. You would do anything to protect this child, even at the expense of your own survival. This new and powerful emotion can be overwhelming.

Depression: Maybe you're also feeling depressed. Postpartum depression is a difficult experience. In new moms, the depression is almost always hormonally based. In new dads, feelings of depression can come from that jolt of reality—with a new baby comes more responsibility, both physically and financially.

Fear: The first few months of parenthood are filled with fears. Will you be able to protect your baby? Will you always know what is best for her? Will you be a good mother? A good father? These are normal, valid concerns, and some of these fears will fade over time. As your parenting skills increase, you will become more confident in your decision-making and learn to trust your instincts.

You've heard the expression: Change is good. Now it's time to live by that expression. Babies change everything. Your lives will be different now—different but *better*. So forget about the fears and anxieties that come along with change. Focus on the miracle that this new being has brought into your lives. Think about that the next time your newborn falls asleep on your chest.

6.

Power Struggles

Most parents first experience a child's attempts at autonomy at around age two. It's at this point that the child feels challenged, and often a battle of wills begins that can last throughout childhood and well into the teen years. Try turning these difficult times into a rewarding growth period for all involved by shifting your perspective and by becoming clever and creative in your responses.

At around age two, children begin individuating from their parents and the world around them. They insist on making decisions for themselves, getting their way, and declaring ownership and authority. This isn't necessarily a bad thing! Parents should view this behavior as a healthy sign of their child's development. Instead of overpowering the child—which can cause young children to feel powerless and in turn seek to hurt others—look at this struggle for power as a positive sign, and reduce the arguing between you and your child.

Avoid asking questions that can be answered with a "no." Try tackling nap time this way: "Do you want to take your nap with your baby doll or your kitty?" "Do you want to lay your head on this end of the bed or the other?" By giving your children choices, you are offering some control over the situation. They will feel as if they have the power, not as if you are exerting your power over them.

Knowing ahead of time where the power struggles between you and your children occur can help you to simply avoid them. By giving your children more power in certain decision-making situations, such as putting on seatbelts, going to bed, or brushing teeth, you're making them feel good about tasks they hate doing. By giving them options, you're making them feel special and loved.

7.

Your Frustrated Preschooler

Preschoolers want what they want, and they almost always want it *now*. For those of you with preschoolers, this comes as no surprise. And it should also come as no surprise that when they can't get what they want, they go berserk.

When a child is frustrated, stress hormones start to flow through the bloodstream and build until they interfere with your child's ability to think straight. Look out—this is when your little angel is most likely to display all sorts of lovely behavior like biting, hitting, screaming—or even screaming "I hate you!"

Obviously, it's important for children to learn that they can't always have their way. With your loving, gentle, compassionate help, you can help your child handle frustration and avoid becoming agitated and upset.

Learn to recognize the early warning signs that set your preschooler off. Is it when you won't buy candy? Avoid the candy aisle completely. Is it when the building blocks keep falling? Get a set specifically designed for three-to four-year-olds, and set your child up in a corner optimal for block building.

Learn what calms your child down. It may mean distracting her from the frustrating situation, or it may mean taking a break from the activity completely. Removing her gently from the situation and suggesting another activity she also enjoys will help.

Creating rules in advance can help, too—believe it or not, preschoolers actually *like* having rules to follow. Write them down, and display them prominently: ICE CREAM IS FOR AFTER DINNER ONLY or NO CANDY AT THE SUPERMARKET. Of course, most kids won't be able to read the rules, but if they hear them often enough, they'll remember what they are and will learn to follow them. Before you set foot in a toy store or the supermarket, go over the rules with your children so that they know you will not be buying them toys or candy inside.

You can't shield your kids from every frustrating situation (you do want them to learn to work through difficulties and accomplish tasks on their own), but taking a little time to explain can certainly ease their frustration levels. It may mean having to slow down and show your daughter how to tie her shoes—even though you're late for an appointment and know it's going to take a while. But time and patience will help your children figure things out for themselves and eventually eliminate their feelings of frustration.

8.

Because I Said So

It happens around the time your child turns two, when he is doing things you never dreamed of. Stuffing small toys or food into the VCR or practicing "scissors skills" on your important mail will elicit responses that have been etched on your brain from about the time you were two: "Wait until your father gets home," "Life isn't fair," or the infamous "Because I said so."

As parents, you frequently make decisions your children don't like. Your children most probably demand to know the reasons for your decisions, and many times, you can try to explain yourself until you're blue in the face. How can you avoid these exasperating arguments? End them before they begin by responding to "But why?" with "Because I said so."

All children cling to the idea that the world should treat them specially. Your job, as a parent, is to set your children straight. Naturally, your kids will not like many of the decisions you make—but they don't have to like them.

Reasoning with young children is one mistake many parents make. It's okay to tell your child why he can't eat dinner in the bathtub, but don't try to persuade him into thinking your reasons have merit. He could care less if his chicken nuggets get wet with dirty bath water. Stick to your decision.

Of course, you'll cringe when you hear the actual words coming out of your mouth: "Because I said so!" You'll remember how, as a kid, you hated to hear those words that prevented you from doing so many things that you wanted to do. But take heart. After saying it about a dozen times, you'll come to realize the truth: Your mother and father knew what they were doing!

9.

Please, Thank You, and Go Away!

It's utterly embarrassing when your six-year-old answers an adult's question of, "Did you have fun on your vacation?" with, "Duh!" But before you yell at your child to apologize, remember that children often do not mean to insult or hurt others with what they say.

To avoid embarrassing situations, it's important to teach your children good manners from the start, and to reinforce this proper behavior continuously. All parents enforce good manners with their preschoolers ("Say thank you to Mrs. Woods," or "Say please to the ice cream man"), but as your children get older, they need to learn appropriate manners for dealing with adults beyond saying please or thank you. Children ages four and older should begin learning the proper way to speak to adults.

As annoying as your children's lack of manners can be, resist the urge to reprimand them in front of others. Lead them away and quietly correct them. Show them that you love them for being so friendly and eager to share their feelings, but that when they're speaking to adults, they must remember to be polite. Your children may not be aware of their bad manners. When a child gives a rude response to another adult, as in the situation above, ask her if that's the way she would have responded if her teacher had asked her about her vacation. Offer her a "correct" response that she could have given instead, such as, "Yes! I had a lot of fun on my vacation." Tell her that people like it when she answers them politely, and that saying "Duh!" might hurt their feelings.

Obviously, with younger children, getting into the habit of saying please and thank you is the best way you can lead them on the path to good manners later on. Always praise your children for using good manners—believe it or not, children often feel embarrassed when they use such "adult" expressions as "How are you?" and "Fine, thank you." It makes them feel silly when they say these same expressions themselves. Teach them to realize the difference between being silly and being polite.

Overall, the only way to instill good manners in your children is to use them yourself. In advance of a social situation, brief your children on what manners will be expected of them. Try role-playing at home to give your kids a preview of what they might expect in certain social situations. And always encourage your kids to be polite—even with their friends on the playground! Rest assured, the day will come when you overhear your child speaking politely to another adult.

10.

Sophisticated Baby Talk

More often than not, parents find themselves talking in cutesy baby talk. It just happens; you can't help it. You could kick yourself for speaking that way, but sometimes when you're trying to get through to your children, using the baby talk you know they understand is just more—well, convenient. And though it may be irritating for you or the casual bystander to hear, it's important to speak to your children in a language that they understand.

Babies are primed to learn speech, and starting as early as possible is the best way parents can help their children develop language. But how, exactly, should you talk to your baby? Tone is more important than the actual terms. Making eye contact and speaking in simple terms and expressive tones help your baby learn to communicate early on. Try not to use too many nonsensical words—use words your baby can learn to understand. Speak with short utterances and repetition to help your child to remember words: Receptive language develops long before expressive language.

Most experts also agree that though baby talk may get the reaction you're looking for from your little one, it's important to increase your level of communication as your baby grows. Language milestones differ from child to child, and children move at their own pace. You can't force your son to begin speaking at 18 months old, but you should be on top of things should he still not be speaking closer to age two. Seek professional advice if you notice your child's speech development is lagging or if you think there may be a problem with his hearing.

11.

Traditional Role Reversal

One important thing to remember as a parent is that breaking away from tradition has many positive advantages for your children. For example, a mother who shares her traditional feminine skills of cooking and gardening with her son helps to balance the emphasis society puts on sports and winning for boys. And a father who encourages his daughter to play Little League is helping to promote her independent thinking and assisting her in overcoming more passive female stereotyping.

It's never easy, especially when kids' peers can be so ruthless. A young boy who favors baking brownies over playing touch football after school could be subjected to ridicule. But moms can help integrate his hobbies. Baking brownies to share with his teammates will certainly be appreciated. Encouraging your son to balance or combine his interests will help him feel better about himself and his hobbies.

Young girls have it just as tough. Even today, after decades of protesting, there are still very few girls joining community Little League programs, and only a handful of organized sports offered at school for girls. While it's rare to see a ponytail hanging from the back of a baseball cap during a Little League game, it isn't for lack of trying. Girls and their mothers have been rallying for years to be allowed to play with the boys. The best thing a father can do to empower his daughter is to lend all the support he can—by spearheading the rally to get her a place on the team and making it one of his top priorities. When dad's on her side, fighting for her cause, she knows her interests are as important to him as they are to her.

Breaking tradition is important for younger children, too. So often we see the father of a two-year-old boy on a play date cringe when his son chooses to play with a toy vacuum or shopping cart. And how many times do we see mothers buying countless Barbies for their daughters—dolls which end up sitting in their boxes unopened? Children need to be encouraged to play with the toys they find interesting and fun—whether it be a toy soldier set for Kathy or a tea set for Jordan. Whichever toys your children pick up at this stage can only broaden their experiences and help them learn. A balanced child whose life is broadened by a variety of experiences will develop more empathy for others and a better sense of self down the road. Think about it this way: Your son who favors the homemaking corner at preschool may grow up to be the next four-star chef. And your toddler daughter who would rather run around the yard than have a tea party with her dolls may grow up to be the next superstar athlete.

12.

Taking Your Children
in Public

It's inevitable: There will come a time when you'll have to take your children out in public. If you're headed out shopping with your children, you're headed for a stressful situation. So here's a plan you can use to deal with your children in any public setting—and to help them learn the value of self-control at the same time.

What you should not do is bribe your kids. Yes, it's a quick solution to an "I want candy!" enraged tantrum. But resort to bribery now, and you'll pay dearly for months—maybe years—to come.

Instead, tell your children the purpose of your outing in advance so that they know exactly what to expect. "We have no milk at home, and I know how you love chocolate milk in the morning, so we need to buy some in this store. We're not going to buy toys or candy in this store. Even if you see toys or candy in this store, I am not buying toys or candy." Don't promise your children toys or candy if they behave in a store; that will teach them to expect rewards simply for behaving well. Save yourself a lot of grief by teaching your children that they shouldn't expect goodies every time the family goes shopping. Teach them to expect only the basic necessities. That way, they'll never acquire the habit of constantly pleading for stuff during shopping trips.

Explain to your children a few short rules before going into the store: "Stay with me, talk quietly, no fighting, and don't touch anything." When these rules are broken—and they will be broken!—immediately take your children aside and straighten them out. Avoid aisles where toys and candy are sold.

You should also avoid taking your children shopping anywhere near mealtime or naptime. Outings can easily overstimulate kids, and setting out with a well-fed, well-rested child will serve you well.

If a situation does come up, and your child starts screaming or acting out of control, go quickly to a remote part of the store, and stay there until the tantrum subsides. The quicker you stop the momentum of your child's misbehavior, the better.

If things don't improve, and your child is hysterical with no end in sight, take the child out of the store for a while. This goes for a restaurant, as well. Leave the scene of the crime, and retreat to the car for the remainder of the tantrum. Abandoning a shopping cart of groceries or a restaurant table of food to regain control over your child may seem drastic, but it works. As soon as your child understands what is expected in public, your outings will become less like chores and more like adventures for both of you.

13.

"I Love You!"

The first time your child says, "I love you," you realize that without knowing it, you've been waiting to hear those words. Is any statement more meaningful, or necessary, between a parent and child? In many families, these words come easily. But if you never heard them growing up, or if members of your family used them to manipulate, it may feel unnatural saying them to your own kids.

Saying "I love you" should not be reserved for special occasions. Your children need to hear it—from both parents—at least once a day. Make sure you say the actual words often! Don't assume that your children know you love them. If you're somebody who has trouble saying the words, practice whispering them first—maybe into your newborn's ear while she sleeps. Or try writing them on a little piece of paper and slipping them into your child's lunchbox or on top of her pillow.

"I love you" is a powerful statement, and most of the time, it will invoke a loving response from the recipient. Try to avoid attaching these feelings to a behavior. "I love you when you clean up your room" suggests that you love your children because of their behavior or accomplishments. Another thing to avoid is saying "I love you" as a precursor to your reaction to something your children have done that you don't approve of. Hearing "I love you, but I can't give you a snack because you didn't finish dinner" is confusing to your children.

The bottom line is to keep it plain and simple. Say "I love you" to your child because you want to say it—because you feel love toward your child, and because it feels good to say it. More often than not, you'll hear it said back!

14.

When Your Children
Are Less Than Loving

After all of the love you've given, after all of the hugs and kisses, presents and gifts, birthday parties thrown and play dates hosted, after the trips to the doctor and the endless comforting, there will come a day when your precious, thoughtful, loving child says those three words that will sting harsher than a hive full of bees: "I hate you!"

Nothing can trigger anger, shame, resentment, shock, and helplessness faster than this statement from your child. Is it true? Does he really hate you? No, of course not. He most likely hates the fact that you won't let him eat gum for breakfast or let him go to the year's best high school party. But whether you realize this or not—that your child is only speaking out of anger and frustration—it's still hard to hear someone you love tell you that he hates you. It's even harder to keep from taking it personally!

Your children know this—they learn it at an early age. When

they say, "I hate you," they get a lot of bang for the buck! Your reaction, although negative, is instant attention. They may also realize that after an "I hate you," you are so riled up, angry, and hurt that you'll give into their demands in the end, if only they'll say they didn't mean it.

It's easy to fall into despair and go on and on to your children about how sad they made Mommy, or how Daddy's heart is broken, but that places a heavy burden on your children—at any age. It implies that your kids are responsible for your feelings. Instead, acknowledge the feelings behind the statement. Tell him, "You sound pretty mad," or "I felt that way when I was a kid, too."

If you've been hurt by an "I hate you!" from your child, the best thing you can do is to refrain from saying anything hurtful. Remove yourself from the situation, walk into the living room, sit on the couch, take a few deep breaths—maybe call your spouse for some encouragement, reassurance, and understanding. Leave the door open for further discussions with your child at a later, calmer time: "We'll talk about this later when we're not so angry."

When your child says, "I hate you," he is trying to push your buttons and get attention. But remember to keep your perspective—you may be hated for a moment or two, but your child is only looking for a reaction from you. Keep your cool, and he'll learn that saying "I hate you" won't get that reaction. Then he won't be able to use this statement to manipulate you in the future.

15.

Let 'Em Win...

Sometimes

How many times have you listened to your spouse argue with your three-year-old over wearing her pajama top outdoors? It's amazing to watch an intelligent, rational adult reduced to saying such unintelligent, irrational things as, "You'll freeze to death in that pajama top!" or "Nobody at the playground will play with you in those clothes!"

Debating with a toddler on such topics as indoor/outdoor weather differences or appropriate day and night clothing is exasperating, but all parents get suckered into it at least once a day. Of course, it isn't appropriate for people to leave the house in their pajamas, but when the "people" we're referring to are the five-and-under set, not only is it appropriate, it's highly common! Sure, it irks you to no end—all you can think about are the stacks of nice new clothes that remain untouched in her dresser while you glare at the threadbare pajama top. But when it comes to a battle such as this, there's really only one thing you can do: Give up, and let her wear the pajamas.

Consider the countless other battles you and your child may have during the course of the week. In all likelihood, most of these arguments, for kids, are nonnegotiable: They'll never win them. As parents, take a moment to realize that consistently losing battles simply has to be frustrating for them. You've no doubt heard the phrase "Pick and choose your battles" when it comes to raising children. It's at times like these, when no harm can really come from wearing a pajama top to the playground, that it's a good idea to take a dive and lose the battle. Let her win. Go a step further, and declare her the winner. This is what's known as a "win-win" situation: She'll think she's won, and you'll know you've won.

Children who are constantly overpowered by their parents and teachers will often seek to hurt others in order to vent their own frustrations. But by "throwing the fight" every once in a while, you'll make them feel good about themselves and eventually help them become self-reliant, self-confident adults who can make good decisions on their own.

16.

A Recipe for Peace

It's ten minutes before dinner, and your four-year-old skips into the kitchen, hungry and asking for a cookie. When you try to explain that dinner will be ready in a few moments, a tantrum ensues. Your child is "starving right now!"

It's futile to argue with a child who's in the middle of a tantrum. Instead of getting through to the youngster, you will likely upset him even more. That in turn makes the child feel miserable and makes you feel ineffectual.

So next time (and you know there will be a next time), just stop talking after you tell your child that dinner will be ready in a few minutes. When the child realizes that you're not going to argue, he may skip any begging and pleading and jump right into the full-fledged tantrum. This may ruin dinner and the rest of your evening. So you can do one of two things to keep the peace in your kitchen: You can give in and give the child a cookie, which will tell your child that it's okay to throw a tantrum in order to get what he wants, or you can take steps to avoid the tantrum completely. Here's one

45

efficient way that almost always works with young children.

Before you begin dinner, make sure there are ample healthy snacks set within your children's reach, arranged in an attractive and enticing way. For instance, before you start anything that has to do with dinner, concentrate on your kids' appetites. Cut up some cucumbers, celery, grapes, cheese cubes, baby carrots, and apples, and arrange them on a big platter. Add a few breadsticks or rice cakes, and place the platter within reach of your youngest child. Set out a few glasses of water and announce to your kids that it's snack time.

Chances are that if you prepare a tasty snack for your children before they realize they're hungry, they're more likely to eat what you've prepared rather than asking for other foods. Children know what they like to eat, but if you wait until hunger sets in before feeding them, they're going to demand what they know they like—immediately. Asking them to wait for dinner to finish cooking when they're hungry "right now" won't fly with even the most patient children.

Now, let's say you present your snacks to your children, and as you're preparing dinner, they polish them off and are no longer hungry. Great! A plateful of vegetables, fruit, cheese, and breadsticks is just as healthy as a plateful of chicken and rice, for example, and a much healthier dinner than many parents fix for their kids on most nights. You and your spouse can now sit down to eat your dinner in peace and quiet. Put the leftovers away for another night.

17.

Catch the Exercise Bug

Studies have shown that the average child (ages 6 to 11) watches 25 hours of television a week. That's not even taking into consideration the countless additional hours kids are playing video games and using their computers. The shocking news is in: Only about one-half of young Americans participate regularly in vigorous physical activity. American children today are more obese than ever—with inactivity highest among young girls.

Inactive children grow up to be inactive adults, so the best time to foster a healthy, active lifestyle is in childhood, when lifelong habits are more likely to develop. Help your children turn those 25 hours in front of the tube into 25 hours of physical fun!

Your kids are more apt to engage in physical activities if you participate with them. Look for activities you can do together, like swimming, biking, ice skating, or playing basketball in the driveway. Or turn your regular daily activities into mini-workouts: Encourage your children to take stairs instead of elevators, or make a game out of parking in the space farthest away from where you are doing errands. Race them to the mailbox or take them with you on your early morning walks. For your daughter's next birthday, buy her a volleyball net or a basketball hoop. The next time that you need a gift for your son, buy him in-line skates (don't forget the helmet and kneepads). As the parent, it's up to you to make the best healthy choices for your children. Consider the results: Regular physical activity enhances both physical and mental health, increases positive feelings about body image, and improves self-esteem and self-confidence.

18.

Raising Kids Who Care

It's always amazing to read about kids from all corners of the country who become so moved by the plight of others that it propels them to actively try to help. After learning that big drug companies send hundreds of thousands of free drug and medication samples to local doctors and hospitals every day, a teenage boy in New York devised a way to collect these samples and ship them to the sick and needy in South America. After meeting a child with a life-threatening illness, a four-year-old girl in California organized a beanbag animal collection within her preschool class, and then sent the stuffed toys to a local hospital children's ward.

Many parents feel that they need to shield their children from the social and personal problems of the world, but in fact, the best thing parents can do is open their children's eyes to these problems in an age-appropriate way. Children have not yet had the chance to become desensitized to the ills of the world. Exposing them to homeless or neglected children, pollution, or people with life-threatening illnesses may motivate them to do something to help.

With younger children, be on the lookout for those "teachable moments" when you can help your children put themselves in another's shoes. If your daughter is not sharing her toys with a playmate, take a second to explain the principle of fairness. Read books about sharing and being kind to others to your children, and start a small change collection in a piggy bank for "children whose mommies and daddies can't afford to buy them nice toys." With older kids, talk about public issues in ways that make it clear people can do something about them. Animal rights, violence in our schools, the rain forest—your children will almost always surprise you by offering a multitude of suggestions on how to help.

Nobody wants to upset their kids unnecessarily. You must know your own children and gauge how they will react to different issues. But if you don't talk about the world's problems with your children, these troubling issues may eventually overwhelm them and make them feel powerless. Plus consider what the experts have learned about socially active children: They are not only more likely to become compassionate citizens but also to excel in school, avoid drugs and alcohol, and be creative problem solvers!

Of course, everyone wants their kids to be caring and responsible, but often, people don't do volunteer work themselves because their lives are just too busy. Taking time to help the less fortunate once a week—or even once a month—will have an enormous impact on your kids. Bringing a child to a soup kitchen or to clean up a local park is one of the best things a parent can do.

Even collecting and recycling cans with your kids can be the perfect way to begin a small fund for the charity of your child's choice. Children who help others in small ways—like recycling cans, giving away old toys when they get new ones, or collecting canned goods or coats for the needy—become more receptive to helping others in need when they become adults.

19.

Bedtime—or More
Simply Put, Armageddon

Ah, bedtime. Before kids, it used to mean a quiet, peaceful time to reflect and gather your thoughts before drifting off to sound slumber; a relaxing time for you and your spouse where days were reviewed and plans were discussed.

If you're the proud parent of a young person, you already know how far from reality that bedtime scenario is. "I want a drink! I need to go to the bathroom! I want a pretzel! I want another kiss! Turn the light on!" Exhausted and frustrated, Mommy and Daddy respond with water, snacks, kisses, and many a trip to the bathroom. Even after all is done, there is always another request: "I'm thirsty again!"

Look at this same scene through the eyes of your child: Your son is playing quietly with blocks, when along you come to rip him away from his play. Imagine that you are in the middle of a good book, and your spouse says, "Time for bed!" Despite your pleas for a few more minutes, you are pulled from the sofa, dragged upstairs, dressed in pajamas, and put to bed. Are you feeling violated? Angry? Controlled?

Your child, though only two, feels all those feelings. At this important growth stage of wanting independence, he's on the verge of becoming an individual. Going to bed may not even be the issue for him—he's most likely tired and ready for sleep—but the continuing commands, being told what to do and when to do it, bring up a feeling of being controlled.

Set a bedtime for your child, and have him commit it to memory. Most importantly, give your child a 45-minute warning before his actual bedtime—so he'll know it's time to start winding down but that he still has a little more time to share with you before lights out.

Include both parents in your child's bedtime ritual. Let the child take part in the ritual—give him choices so that he'll feel more important and less controlled. "Do you want Mommy or Daddy to help you put on your pajamas?" "Do you want to wear your baseball pajamas or your frog pajamas?"

Give him a final warning at 15 minutes before lights out, and use the remaining time to snuggle or read to your child. Include the number of books, songs, or kisses into the routine so that he'll always know the rule: two books, two songs, and five kisses before lights out. Finally, explain to him once that after the last kiss, you are going to say good-night and leave the room.

This may not work the first time, but it's important that you be consistent. Try not to speak to your child after the bedtime routine is complete. If he comes out of his room, quietly guide him back. You don't want to begin a verbal power struggle about going to bed. Yes, he'll test you a few times in the beginning—maybe getting out of bed six or seven times in one night. But after sticking to this routine for a few nights, bedtime is sure to become more pleasant for you and your child.

20.

Turning Sibling Rivalry
into Sibling Chivalry

Constant fighting between siblings is one of the major frustrations parents have. Parents' reaction to their kids' squabbling almost always includes screaming, taking sides, threats, accusations, and stepping in to solve the problem. When parents react to hostility with hostility, they are unwittingly promoting sibling rivalry. Our children need the skills of negotiation and cooperation in order to succeed as adults. We can begin to teach our kids these important skills now.

Having more than one child can provide opportunities for your kids to learn many things such as how to share, be a friend, get along with others, and cooperate. Instead of reacting to the fighting and bickering that occurs between siblings, parents can choose to stay out of the fights in a nonjudgmental way—provided that the fighting does not get physical. Children need to settle things for themselves, and parents should let them.

Before your children next "go at it," when things are calm and quiet, take the time to teach them the skills they need to work out their problems. Teach them how to negotiate and share, and put them in situations where they can practice these skills. If you leave two-year-old twins in a room with blocks, you're asking for trouble. But if you sit down with them first and divide the blocks, you can demonstrate fair play. You can even teach them how to trade. If you show them that you have confidence in them to work out their problems on their own, you'll be surprised to see that even very young children enjoy being left in charge of their play time.

As your children get older, sibling rivalry usually gets worse, mainly because they become more verbal. The reasons for fighting may change—"She's looking at me!" "He's on my side of the couch!"—but your proactive reaction should stay the same. Even if they repeatedly cry out for your intervention, *do not get involved!* It may take many ear-splitting, nerve-shattering moments for them to come to the realization that you aren't going to step in. But letting your kids settle their differences on their own will help them work the problems out for themselves in the end.

21.

Pencil In Your Kids
for a Family Meeting

Family meetings can be a very successful method of enhancing family closeness, and in a world filled with extracurricular activities, it's easy to go for weeks, or sometimes months, without spending quality time with the people you love. The hardest part of having a weekly family meeting is scheduling a time when everybody is home! But once you decide on the time, make it a priority, and keep it sacred. Mark it on your calendar, and make it as important for you as a business meeting and as important for your kids as dates with their friends. This will show your children how valuable this time is to you and make them feel that you take them seriously.

Keep a list in view for anyone to record problems that may arise during the week. Plan to discuss them during your family meeting time. At meeting time, select a comfortable place where everyone can relax. It isn't a good idea to have this meeting during mealtime—there are too many distractions. In addition, before the meeting begins, take the phone off the hook so that there will be no interruptions.

Elect a new leader and a new recording secretary at each meeting. The leader should run the meeting and call on family members to speak in turn. For each new meeting, select a different leader. The recording secretary should take notes on what is discussed and what decisions are reached.

Make sure to compliment each family member at the start of your meetings—this isn't a time for fighting or ganging up on one person. If you have gripes, air them, and encourage your children to air theirs—but keep them constructive. Remember why you're sitting together: to spend quality time as a family, not to harp on your family's problems. If a family member has a problem to bring up, teach your children that it's helpful to think of a solution.

Always close the meeting by allowing the leader to select a fun way to end it. You can choose to play a board game, bake a family snack together, watch home videos, or plan your next family vacation. However you decide to end your family meeting, always be sure to schedule the next meeting and select a new leader and secretary.

Thousands of families benefit from holding weekly family meetings each year. Some parents say that this is the only time of the week they get the chance to talk to their kids! Remember, whatever it is you do together—baking, playing games, or just shooting the breeze—the main idea is that you're doing it…together!

22.

Empowering Your Kids

Believe it or not, there are endless ways your kids could be valuable to your community. Studies show that the most underused, wasted natural resource in this country is our children! With so many great ideas, so much energy and boundless idealism, their potential to make a difference is limitless.

The key to empowering your children is becoming aware of their strengths early on and giving them a lot of opportunities to put those strengths to use. Is your 11-year-old daughter kind, compassionate, and resourceful? Take her to volunteer at a homeless shelter one day a week. Does your eight-year-old son show concern for the environment? Solicit his help in picking up litter in your neighborhood. There are large and small opportunities every day for children to be valuable, contributing members of society, and the benefits for your kids, your family, and your community are priceless.

A young girl from New York recently celebrated her fifth birthday and instead of asking for presents, she asked for donations to be made to the American Cancer Society. Sadly, this girl had experienced the loss of two family members to cancer, and had a real understanding of how donations from her friends could help others who were sick with cancer. Her decision, in turn, helped 20 other five-year-olds develop a caring attitude about helping others.

There is no better way to support kids in feeling good about themselves than to help them to be of service to others. When we value our children's contributions and input, we're giving them the power to make a difference in their lives and in the lives of others.

23.

Keeping Expectations
to a Minimum

Without even realizing it, we often put pressure on our children. There is pressure to keep from making mistakes, pressure to behave a certain way, and pressure to live up to all of our expectations.

Certain pressures motivate our children to try harder to win our approval. Our intentions may be good, but these pressures may end up pushing our kids too hard. When you say, "My son is the smartest in his class!" or "My daughter got all A's and one B on her report card. Next time, I know she'll get all A's!" you may not be thinking about how your children are interpreting the words. You're praising them, and you're proud of them, but to a nine-year-old, that praise may be interpreted as an expectation. Now the child has to "measure up" to your expectations in order to win the same approval all of the time.

You need to watch what you say in regard to your children's

accomplishments so that they'll always know you're proud of them. It's a good idea to eliminate words like "best" and "brightest" from your vocabulary when you're referring to your children. Your kids need to be able to look at you and always see unconditional love and pride, to know that they are loved because of who they are, and not for what they do or how they look.

It's a tough, competitive world out there, and the pressure on your kids in the new millennium is unprecedented. It is your job to instill in your children feelings of pride, self-respect, and accomplishment, no matter where they are on the traditional scales of "success." In doing so, you show them that you love them for who they are, not just what they can do.

24.

Raising Children
with Morals

There are two simple ways you can accomplish teaching morals and values to your kids. The first is to give your child on-the-spot lessons in honesty. Nearly every day, something happens that presents a chance for you to do this. For example, your four-year-old has just walked out of the toy store with a Hot Wheels car you didn't buy. You notice the car in his hand as you are buckling him into his safety seat. He has a guilty expression on his face—you get the feeling knows that he's done something wrong. Here's a good chance to make a lasting impression on him about what's right and what's wrong.

Do not make excuses for your child and laugh it off, saying, "He's only four—he didn't mean to steal it." That may be true—young children don't completely comprehend the notion of stealing—but if you don't deal with what he did, you are letting him know that it's okay to take something that's not his. Hold your child accountable for his actions. Remember to keep the atmosphere loving and non-threatening. Explain to him in a calm manner that you are disappointed in him for taking the toy from the store. Just hearing those words can have a deep effect on your child. Further explain that taking the car was wrong and that he needs to return it to the store manager and apologize immediately.

Another method of teaching your children to have morals is to simply set a good example for them. Opportunities for setting an example present themselves all the time. Your job is to seek them out and act upon them in a productive manner.

Let's say that you're going to the store with your first-grader, and you spot a ten-dollar bill on the ground in the parking lot. Your daughter sees it, too, and rushes to pick it up. True, you'll probably never find the person who dropped the money. But resist the urge to proclaim this your lucky day, and instead, ask your daughter what would happen if she had been the one who had lost the money. Would she feel sad? Would she return to the parking lot to search for the money? Chances are that she'll answer yes to both questions and feel some compassion for the person who dropped the money. Ask her what she thinks you should do with the money. Offer some suggestions of your own. Leaving the money where you found it or with a nearby store owner may sound like worthless attempts, but you will have taught your daughter a valuable lesson about compassion and honesty. In the long run, that's worth more than ten dollars!

25.

Cheat Sheet for Happiness

Good parents want to discipline their children in a way that teaches responsibility and builds their children's self-esteem. We want them to feel loved and happy, even though we may need to punish them occasionally. If our children are disciplined in this respect, they will not have a need to turn to gangs, drugs, or other methods of rebellion to feel powerful or belong. There are some very simple ways to give your children a sense of well-being and security:

Be sure to spend quality time with your child. Set aside time for you and your children to spend together—other than the time you spend dragging them around town to run errands. It's not the amount of time that's important; it's the quality of time. During this time, give them your undivided attention.

Your actions will speak louder than words. Studies have shown that parents make as many as 2,000 requests of their children every day. It is your job to teach your children how to grow up and develop responsibility. Repeating yourself over and over is part of this job. But it helps to back those words up with action. If you've nagged your son continuously about putting his dirty clothes in the hamper, next time you do the laundry, just wash what he's put in the hamper. Yes, it may be frustrating if he complains that he has no clean clothes, but he's not going to understand the importance of your request unless he sees just how his actions affect his own situation.

Give them the power. Give your children some control by allowing them to help with grownup chores. Often we do things for our kids, because we can do them more easily or more quickly. That only results in their feeling unimportant and useless.

Don't butt in. When you interfere, you rob children of the chance to learn from the consequences of their actions. If your daughter forgets her show-and-tell project for kindergarten, don't rush home for it—let the consequences teach her a lesson about the importance of remembering.

Let the punishment fit the crime. In the heat of the moment, sometimes you may be tempted to slap on a ridiculous sentence for a petty crime. Say you're headed into the house with your arms full of packages, and your youngest begins to wail. Your oldest is responsible—she took his toy, or something to that effect. The stress associated with holding the heavy bags and fumbling for your house keys, combined with the irritating sound of crying, can set you off on a punishing rampage. Don't send her to her room for the rest of the night. When your cooler head prevails, explain to her why she should not take things away from others.

Be consistent. This is actually the most important key to effective parenting. Inconsistency is completely ineffective. Your son is on a play date, and he hits another child. Reprimand him and explain that if he hits again, you'll take him home. If he does it again, pack him up and leave—even if it's inconvenient. It's never easy to stick to your guns with a threat or a punishment, but the second that you give in, you lose all credibility.

26.

It's the Little Things
That Count

Sometimes it's the small, relatively painless ways you interact with your kids that can make the biggest improvements in your family life—ways for any parents to strengthen the bonds between them and their children.

Read to your kids at bedtime. Sharing stories will bring you closer and help them develop a love for books and a desire to read.

Praise your children as often as possible. In our busy lives, we often take for granted the good behavior that our kids display. We're always on the lookout to reprimand them for their bad behavior. Praising your children for nice things that they do teaches them not to take others' kindness for granted.

Cut down on extracurricular activities. Does your child really need art and gymnastics classes, swimming and piano lessons, and soccer? Most children in the United States today are wildly overscheduled. Try cutting down on just one activity, and use that time to share a quiet, fun activity at home with her.

Kiss and hug and kiss and hug. Or hold hands, or tickle, or play with your child's hair. Expressing your feelings with physical gestures can brighten your child's day.

Leave them be. It's hard, sometimes, to keep from following your five-year-old around the playground. Of course, you must keep him in sight at all times, and if an apparatus presents a danger, you have to stay close. But if the play equipment is safe and age-appropriate, it's healthier to let children explore on their own.

Laugh as much as possible. You can create an atmosphere of joy and happiness for you and your child if you make an effort to smile and laugh more when you're together. Research also shows that young children mirror our expressions—so if you're smiling, your child will smile, too. With older kids, just having Mom or Dad laugh at one of their jokes can make their day.

Be silly. Too many parents are bothered or irritated when their kids act silly in public. Preschoolers especially enjoy talking silly, using bathroom words, or just making faces. There's nothing wrong with joining them on their level and sharing their funny moments. And kids should never be told to stop being silly, unless they are also being disruptive or silly at inappropriate times such as during school.

Raising children can be an overwhelming job. Remember that enormous changes for the better begin with tiny steps. Try putting just one of these steps into practice this week, and with that step, you'll already have begun the process of change!

27.

Stress Busters

"Nap when your baby naps." Anybody ever give you that piece of advice? Did they also have any other pearls of wisdom to offer, such as if you're napping with baby, how you are supposed to do the laundry, clean the house, prepare the baby's bottles, fix dinner, or venture outdoors?

Chances are that unless you have a baby nurse, a nanny, a cleaning service, and a personal assistant, you're not doing any napping while baby naps. If you do, you can bet that your house and the world around you will quickly sink into disarray. A new parent lives in a state of constant sleep deprivation. If you've got other children to take care of in addition to the baby, or maybe you're holding down a job, as well, you're exhausted, anxious, and overwhelmed.

Unfortunately, you may never get the chance to really relax until your baby is grown and out of the house. But you *can* rework your present days to include some sporadic energy boosters and some de-stressing techniques to help you wind down and sleep better at night.

Begin your day by getting in a workout. It's a fact that being active increases your adrenaline, which gives you more energy. A 15-minute workout within the confines of your own home can be enough to recharge your batteries. Lifting hand weights or stretching with an exercise video can do wonders to increase your energy level.

Get some fresh air. If the weather is nice, pop the baby in her stroller and head outside—if for nothing else than to give yourself a change of scenery.

Light some candles! Aromatherapists recommend rosemary, pine, or citrus to relieve mental fatigue and stimulate your system.

Keep in touch with your friends. Talking to a friend during the day—even if it's while you're nursing or preparing a meal—can give you a real burst of energy. It can help keep you alert and active and make you feel connected to the real world.

When it's time to wind down, make sure to create a quiet, peaceful atmosphere. Of course, that may not always be possible. If your baby is still awake, hand her over to your spouse, and give yourself a break. Grab a good book or magazine—provided it isn't about anything that will produce anxiety—and settle into your favorite chair. Treat yourself to a snack rich in carbohydrates, which stimulate the brain chemicals that help you sleep soundly.

A hot bath will also works wonders for relaxing you and your baby—just be sure that the water isn't too hot. Elevating your body temperature before bedtime is perfect because the after-bath cooldown helps induce sleep.

Lower the lights, avoid other sensory stimulation such as loud music, television, or computers, and if baby has called it quits for the day, go to sleep! Even if it's only for a few hours, beginning your sleep with a proper wind-down may make all the difference in lowering your levels of stress.

28.

Listen to the Experts

Often, the best child-rearing advice comes from one of the most knowledgeable experts around: your mother. Or your best friend. Or your cousin. That's because when it comes to hands-on experience, tried-and-true methods of child rearing almost always work best. You can only learn these secret methods from someone who has done the parenting thing—sometimes twice over.

Words of wisdom—from wherever they come—can change your life. While it's not always practical to call your pediatrician every time you have a question or to hit the library when you need professional advice, you can always get the word out to your network of new-parent friends with a phone call or e-mail.

Here are some quick words of wisdom randomly selected from new parents across the country. Keep them handy—even the ones you think you have no use for now.

Don't tiptoe while the baby is sleeping. You want her to learn how to sleep in somewhat noisy situations so that you'll be able to live like a regular person while she naps without fear of waking her up.

Pick up your baby as much as you want. Some people warn that picking up your baby too much can spoil her. It's simply not true. You can't spoil an infant.

Write everything down. You don't have to keep a formal "baby book," but keep a record of what your kids do and say so that you won't forget.

Trust your instincts. Many new parents are hesitant to call the pediatrician after hours. Remember that pediatricians expect late-night calls, and it's always better to be safe than sorry.

Freeze breast milk in plastic ice cube trays. When the milk is frozen, empty the cubes into labeled freezer bags for quick and easy measurement. This also cuts down on wasted milk, since you only have to thaw what you need.

Install your infant car seat while you're still expecting the baby. Practice putting it in and taking it out. Taking your baby home for the first time can be stressful enough without having to figure out how a car seat works.

Never believe your children when they say they don't have to go. This is the best piece of advice ever! Traditionally, little boys can hold it in longer, but little girls especially have to visit the bathroom often! So the next time you're headed out, before you start that car ride, sit down at a restaurant, or take your seats at a ballgame, make sure they go—because as soon as you hit the highway, or your food comes, or the first pitch is thrown, you can bet that all of a sudden, they'll have to!

29.

Organize Your Life

It's the most frustrating thing in the world to realize that you have become one of those "unorganized" people that you used to look down upon. Before your baby was born, you prided yourself on your organizational skills, your knack for remembering details and dates, and your ability to keep your home in order.

Then your baby arrived. Suddenly you found yourself without milk, soap, or stamps. You've forgotten your spouse's birthday and your anniversary, and once you even forgot to pick up your older child from baseball practice. Your cell phone charger has been missing for months.

Don't despair. There is hope. With the proper skills, you can get back to your former organized self.

Begin each day by taking five or ten minutes to write down anything and everything you need to do or remember. Organizing your day on paper helps you set priorities—which can save you hours of confusion later on. Include a checklist so that things don't pile up. Put *everything* on that checklist, including the smaller things like replacing a roll of toilet paper. It's amazing what new moms and dads have the capability of forgetting!

Posting an enormous calendar in your kitchen sounds like something other people do. But hanging a dry-erase board on your fridge can help get yourself and your family organized. Write down everything—soccer games, birthday parties, play dates—whatever activities your children are involved in. The objective is to be able to look at any given day and know what's going on.

Ask for help—not only from your spouse, but from your older children! A five-year-old can set the table and an eight-year-old can work the dryer. Older siblings can help younger ones zip up, button up, pour milk, or brush teeth. Enlist everyone's help when the tasks of your day become overwhelming.

If you can multitask, you've got it made. With the baby in a Snuggli, you'll be surprised at how much you can accomplish. You can fold laundry, load the dishwasher, or vacuum with a Snuggli. Multitask whenever humanly possible: Chop veggies for your dinner salad while your son does his homework. Take the baby for a walk while planning your daughter's science project for school. Just don't try doing too many things at once—that may result in getting nothing accomplished.

When you're a new parent, you're constantly wishing you had another pair of hands around the house. But the reality is that there are never enough hands to get everything done! Work with what you've got. Never be ashamed or embarrassed to ask for help.

30.

Don't Baby Bottle
Your Feelings

Marriage experts have always maintained that the first year with a new baby is a tough one for the parents—sometimes literally making or breaking the relationship. When couples become parents, everything changes. Taking care of a child requires a huge developmental leap in the relationship and a greater sense of teamwork—if that's missing, partners are going to drift apart. That's why it's essential to keep on top of your feelings and share them, often and fairly, with your spouse.

With a first baby, everything is always trial and error. You and your spouse must feel your way through your new roles, and you may find yourselves arguing a lot. Discuss your problems and feelings daily to work out the glitches that arise with your new lifestyle change.

You may constantly find yourself learning to juggle your schedules so that the workload is fairly distributed. Experiment with alternative ways to lighten the load: Send out the laundry from time to time, or order dinner in to give you both a break. Perhaps hire a babysitter on weekends so that your child will have company while you and your spouse go out for dinner.

Life with a new baby shouldn't be all about arguing and chores, either. It's essential to make a conscious effort to spend time together as a family and strive to feel appreciation for your spouse. Don't give all of your love and affection to your new baby—save some for your partner.

Most importantly, when the stress takes its toll, let it all out! Don't bottle your feelings—that can only lead to an explosion of anger. It's healthy to complain—everyone does—and even healthier to express your feelings and frustrations. Remember to go about it in a positive way: Instead of accusing, frame your complaints gently: "I really miss spending time with just you," for instance.

Sometimes when there is an issue that can't be resolved by a couple, it's helpful to just let it go. Taking a step back and reviewing the issue from your spouse's perspective may shed some new light on it, bringing you to the realization that the issue is not worth all the aggravation and turmoil. Ultimately, negotiating and tradeoffs are what a successful marriage is all about. The key is to work out the conflict instead of allowing it to escalate.

There's no question about it—it takes patience and a willingness to meet your partner halfway to keep your marriage healthy. But in the end, you can nurture your children and your marriage at the same time if you remember to share your feelings and keep the lines of communication open.

31.

Surviving Separation Anxiety

All children experience anxiety. It's actually expected and normal at specific times in their development. From around seven months through the preschool years, otherwise healthy youngsters may show intense anxiety at times of separation from their parents.

Your child's helpless crying or hysterical tantrums when you leave her at school or with a baby-sitter actually involve profound feelings. Abandonment is a common fear many young children have. Coupled with the anxiety that they have over meeting and talking to new people, leaving them in these situations can sometimes be stressful enough to make them physically ill.

If you know your children become anxious in certain situations, it's important to prepare them beforehand. Children need to experience new people, especially new adults other than their parents. It's important for their social development and for their parents' peace of mind. By keeping your children from growing accustomed to new people, you're creating more anxiety for them down the road.

Before your child's first day of preschool, visit the school beforehand. If possible, have the child meet the teachers and become familiarized with the building and classrooms. Spend some time with your child in the classroom, and pick a spot where you'll say your good-byes every morning and hellos every afternoon. Assure the child that you'll be in that spot every day to bring her home when school is over. Once school begins, it's important to stick to your plans—go through your pre-discussed good-bye routine (three hugs and three kisses), and then leave. There may be tears, and they may come at this moment each day for days or weeks afterward, but ultimately, she'll learn to trust that you will come back for her.

Breaking in a new baby-sitter can be just as stressful unless you prepare properly. Before your first night away with the new sitter in charge, invite the sitter over to "play" and spend time with your child while you're home. Let your child have a good amount of time to become comfortable with this new person—with you close by— and it will diminish her fears of being left alone for the real deal.

It's best to begin separating from your children at an early age—to get them accustomed to new situations and new people, and to determine their levels of anxiety. Early separation will benefit your child enormously, and will benefit you, too, allowing you some healthy time apart from each other.

32.

Raising Unspoiled Kids

Good parenting is not about making sure your children are happy and have everything they need. It's more about helping them learn to deal confidently with setbacks and adversities in life that are inevitable. When you step in to rescue your children from every frustrating situation or give them everything that they want, you're not helping them learn the critical coping skills needed to survive in the adult world.

A big part of raising unspoiled kids is teaching them to consider the needs of others and to put others first sometimes. Emphasize the virtues of concern and kindness with your children. Demonstrate these virtues yourself, and treat every experience as a chance to learn.

As your children grow, they will learn to become self-reliant and independent in many ways—including financially. Supplying your kids with helpful money-managing tips can aid them in learning to live successfully on their own. If they learn to earn money, rather than expecting it from you, only then can they begin to understand the true value of money. While your ten-year-old can't be expected to hold down a nine-to-five job while still in grade school, he can still find odd jobs around the house or around the neighborhood and earn his own money.

Giving your children an allowance can be a powerful tool for teaching them how to manage money. Discuss saving, spending, and charitable giving with them. Allow them to make their own choices about how they spend their money, but always help them understand the ramifications of their choices. Help them to understand the different feelings of satisfaction that come from spending, saving, and donating their money.

Children who are spoiled are children who have never heard the word "no" from their parents. Parents need to make sure the word "no" is part of their vocabulary—and they shouldn't feel guilty for using it. Giving kids what they want, whenever they want it, does not help them learn one of the basic rules of life: You can't always get what you want.

Effective parenting is all about making the right choices that will benefit your kids. That doesn't mean your kids will always like or agree with your choices. But once you make them, stick by them. When your children realize that you are prone to folding like a house of cards, they will quickly learn how to manipulate you in order to get what they want.

33.

Just Who Do Our
Kids Look Up To?

Do our children understand what it means to have character? Do most parents? Considering today's shortage of appropriate role models, it's not hard to understand why it has become more difficult to raise kids with character.

Children best learn about character traits by watching others do things right. Your dilemma lies in the fact that so many of your children's role models send out mixed messages. The very public nature of our society has allowed our children to see behavior that previous generations kept hidden. Your role as parents is to overcome the outside forces that perpetuate immoral, uncaring images, and to raise kids with caring hearts and decent souls.

Dedicated parents need to teach their children strong character traits such as caring, respect, self-control, sharing, tolerance, and fairness. It is our responsibility to nurture the qualities that will enhance their moral growth. We can use the inappropriate choices made by their role models as teaching tools to instill valuable lessons in what kids should not do.

Every day you spend with your children brings a new opportunity to set examples of the proper way to behave in life. When you drive your car, you should be courteous to other drivers. When you order food at a restaurant, you should be polite. You have one valuable advantage over your children's rich and famous role models—you spend a lot more time with your children than they do! It's one thing to talk about how one should live and hope that kids will look up to you. It's another thing entirely to live a good and honorable life in order to set an example for your children.

34.

Teach Right from Wrong

You are the one who has to teach your children the proper moral development. When your kids are learning right and wrong, you're going to have to criticize them from time to time. Your criticism may be constructive, but children can't see that subtlety. After being criticized, they may feel hurt or unloved. That's why it's essential to approach the method with which you develop your children's moral character in a gentle, non-threatening way. You want to offer positive suggestions, but don't want the kids to get defensive or angry.

Special attention should be paid to your children's conduct and attitude toward other people in society. One good way to achieve good conduct is to ask your children to play the underdog in certain situations. "How would you feel if the kids in your class wouldn't let you be in their club?" "How would you feel if you were the one who had to fix the garage window every time you broke it with your ball?" Rather than punishing their wrong or improper behavior, this method helps to build and shape your children's character for the future. As they mature, the decision to follow society's rules and laws ultimately becomes up to them. It's important to help shape a child's moral development at a very young age.

Character is built as a result of parental interaction, balanced discipline styles, and children's own choices. So if you actively begin teaching right from wrong as soon as possible, you can assess your children early on and have a better target for individual development. Hopefully, the end result will be that your children will be the ones who make sure to include others, help someone in need, or resist peer pressure in the future.

35.

Give Her a Boost

Research indicates that girls entering junior high school feel less self-confident than they did in elementary school, and they become less self-confident with each successive year of school. In contrast, the same research shows that boys become more self-confident with each passing year. Parents, teachers, and mentors can have a significant impact on how girls see themselves. By offering the right kind of support, they can potentially avoid many of the common problems rooted in girls' low self-esteem.

Appearance can be a highly sensitive area for young girls. Girls are harshly judged by other girls if they don't fit into society's narrow definition of beauty. As a result, a girl's body becomes the focus of her attention. At its worst, this can lead to eating disorders or a desperate desire for plastic surgery. To help a girl develop a healthier self-image, compliment her on her achievements, thoughts, and actions instead of her hair, makeup, and outfits. Remind her that she is a smart, valuable person with great ideas and a lot of potential.

So many young girls feel so negative about themselves because they are continuously bombarded with picture-perfect images of girls and women on television and in magazines. Expose those images for that they are—retouched, computer-manipulated photos of models—and remind your child that models and actresses are only a very small percentage of the population.

Encourage your daughter to get involved in sports at school. Being on a team or competing in an individual sport is a great way for girls to devote the time and energy they'd normally focus on superficial concerns toward healthy physical activity. Studies also show that girls who participate in sports get better grades than girls who don't. These girls are accustomed to focusing on outer events and on things other than themselves.

Most importantly, encourage your daughter to express her opinions. Research has proven that in the classroom, girls are more frequently interrupted than boys are. Because of this, girls may begin to get the message that what they have to say isn't important. If a girl learns to use her voice confidently and on a regular basis, people will listen to her and respect her. Teach her to be a risk-taker, too. Teachers are more likely to step in and solve problems for girls who are stuck than they are for boys. They reward girls for being good and behaving well, as opposed to being adventurous in their thinking, as boys are. Giving your daughter an opportunity to problem-solve on her own can chart a course for boosting her self-esteem.

36.

The Importance
of Baby-Sitters

Leaving your children with a baby-sitter is important for many reasons. Most obvious among them is that it offers you and your spouse some valuable time to yourselves, without the constant interruptions of tending to the needs of your children. It gives you a chance to eat a meal, sip coffee, or just see a movie without distractions. Of course you love your kids, but sometimes answering their demands can put a heavy strain on your well-being. Before that strain begins to interfere with the quality time you spend with your kids, you should consider hiring a baby-sitter.

Another reason it's important to indulge in a sitter every so often is that it's truly beneficial for your children to interact with adults or teenagers other than you and your spouse. Young children, especially, tend to develop very loving relationships with their baby-sitters—relationships that fulfill needs you or your children's siblings can't.

When selecting a baby-sitter, it's wise to proceed with caution. Always check references when interviewing a prospective baby-sitter. Never leave your children with anyone that you don't know. Ask for three references (unrelated) who know the sitter well and can verify that the sitter is trustworthy, responsible, and qualified to care for children.

Don't underestimate the importance of an interview. You need to spend a good amount of time talking to and getting to know a baby-sitter. Ask direct questions, such as, "Do you have experience with infants?" or "Have you ever cared for two children at once before?" Ask hypothetical questions, too, like what the sitter would do if your child fell and scraped a knee. The baby-sitter you choose should be able to give you a quick and positive answer.

Make sure your baby-sitter knows CPR and first aid, and is physically up to performing them. An accident can happen anytime, even if you are away for a short while. If your baby-sitter doesn't have CPR and first-aid training, insist that he or she obtain it from somewhere. Local community centers and schools often provide this training for a small fee.

To lower the level of separation anxiety your young children may experience, allow them time to get familiarized with the sitter you hire before leaving them alone for the first time. Ask the sitter to come once or twice for a few hours while you are home—then your kids can meet and get to know this sitter in a comfortable atmosphere. (Remember to pay him or her for this time.)

Finally, trust your instincts! Just because a friend used and loved someone doesn't mean that person is right for your kids. You may have reservations about this sitter, or perhaps something about the person rubs you the wrong way. If you have *any* bad feelings about somebody, don't think twice about scratching them off your list of prospects!

Once you hire a sitter, make sure that you communicate all of your important information. Give the sitter a tour of your home and show where everything is: the kids' rooms, the bathrooms, the snacks, the fuse box, the flashlights, the first-aid kit, and of course, a laminated list of all emergency phone numbers.

Choosing the right baby-sitter is a big decision. Taking the time to get to know a sitter and feeling comfortable with your decision will benefit you and your children immensely.

37.

Cut Your Teenager
Some Slack

When your kids become teenagers, they are essentially preparing to separate or individuate from the family. That actual time may be a few years away, but they're already preparing for it. Teens often initiate this separation by rebelling. Teenagers challenge rules and values as a way of establishing their individuality. They now have a heightened need for privacy, thus giving them a sense of control and independence. They're testing out things for themselves, trying to see if they can make the right choices on their own and without you.

Consider the changes teenagers are going through when they do something rebellious or act out in rudeness or insincerity. Hormonal changes can cause mood swings, bouts of crying, heightened sensitivity, and inappropriate laughter. Cut your kids some slack the next time they explode—when all you did was ask what they would like for dinner.

Teenagers also change in the way they relate to the opposite sex. Things are different now. Where there were once friendships, romantic relationships, ambivalence, or even deep, negative emotions can surface. Where your children once felt all-powerful and all-knowing with regard to their place in life and their choices, they are now experiencing new feelings of failure and inadequacy.

So give it some time, and it will pass. You'll have that closeness again—for at least a little while—before they leave the house to go to college or live on their own! For now, if you're desperate for some connection with a teen, wait until he approaches you. When the timing is right, your kid will track you down for some heartfelt one-on-one. In the meantime, just lay low, and don't mention dinner again.

38.

Enjoy Your Kids
Every Single Day

Playing with your children every day is important because it brings you closer to them. But playing is something that's easier for some parents than others. Some parents, though they have the desire and the willingness, just don't have the patience to play with their children. Some may feel uncomfortable getting down on the floor to play, and others may just find it boring to play baby games. It doesn't mean you love your kids less. But if you've been aching to play with your kids and just never acquired the appropriate skills, you can definitely learn everything you need to know to share this close, happy time with your children.

Ask yourself if you enjoy playing with your children, and how often you actually make time to play with them. Are there any obstacles you can foresee that get in the way of play? Devise a system for avoiding these obstacles. Plan your play time ahead of time. Select a thirty-minute slot of time in the day that you can play with the least interruptions. Turn off the television. Take the phone off the hook, or let your machine pick up your calls.

Involve your children by asking them what they would like to play. Parents often decide which toy or board game to play with, but children learn best and play more when they decide what to play and at what pace. More importantly, their concentration, enjoyment level, and good behavior increase as a result! If you absolutely can't make it through another game of Candyland, offer a variety of other fun options for your child to choose instead. Don't try to pretend that you're having fun at a game when you aren't— your child will sense that immediately. Stock your children's toy shelves with fun, interesting games that you can all enjoy.

Next, try flooring it! Even if you aren't the type to get down on the floor for a game of Twister, engaging in this sort of close contact game with your children in a comfortable, informal way will heighten their enjoyment and help you loosen up. Don't be afraid to get crazy and silly if the game calls for it.

Try to keep the praise coming: "That was a great move!" or "Your Lego ship looks great!" Such compliments will help your children learn self-confidence and motivate them to explore further. Best of all, by sitting with them for any activity for a half-hour at a time, you are creating an inevitable closeness with your children and opening the door for communication in a fun, relaxing atmosphere.

39.

Words *Not* to Live By!

Even before your baby is born, you'll be inundated with well-meaning advice from your parents, your in-laws, your neighbors, your doctors, your friends—even strangers at the park. Much of that advice will be right on the mark and greatly appreciated, but a lot of it, however well-intentioned, is going to be nonsense!

A lot of the gems of child-rearing advice passed down from generation to generation are influenced by old wives' tales—many based on false premises that may have, at one time, been thought to be true. Watch out for some of these:

Teething causes fever and diarrhea. If your baby has a fever of more than 101 degrees, call your doctor, even if she is teething up a storm. While teething may cause a low-grade fever, it is not the cause of a high-grade fever which may indicate other problems. Along the same lines, teething and drooling do not cause diarrhea. They may make your baby's stool a little looser than usual, but if your child has bad diarrhea, take her to the doctor.

A drop of baby oil will sooth your baby's ear pain. No! Don't put anything in your baby's ears! Only a doctor can wash out a baby's waxy ears—you should never attempt this at home.

Letting your baby stand on your lap will make him bowlegged. One has nothing to do with the other. Many babies are bowlegged at birth from their position in the womb. If your baby likes to stand on your lap while holding your hands, he's only strengthening his leg muscles.

Your baby will get sick if she's out without a jacket or hat. This is a big misconception. Colds are infections caused by viruses. You cannot catch one by going outside without a jacket. You can only get sick if you are in contact with the infected secretions of other sick people. Getting cold or wet does not weaken the immune system and make you sick. Colds are more frequent in the cold, wet weather because that's when people tend to stay indoors, in closer contact with each other. On the other hand, do dress your children appropriately for cold weather with coats, hats, and gloves.

If you get your baby a walker, he'll learn to walk sooner. Physicians say that the muscles your baby uses to scoot around in a walker are different from the muscles used to walk. Therefore, getting a walker for your baby is not going to help him walk any sooner than if you never put him in one. Many doctors caution parents against buying walkers, since there have been many instances where babies in walkers get injured falling down stairs. If you enjoy having your baby upright and moving, look for a "walker" that is stationary.

Alcohol in your child's bath will lower her fever. When your child has a high fever, giving her a lukewarm bath plus some form of acetaminophen or ibuprofen can help lower it. You should never put alcohol in your baby's bath or rub her down with alcohol, because the alcohol can be absorbed through the skin and cause problems.

Give your baby solid food if you want him to sleep through the night. Introducing solid foods to a baby younger than four months can be potentially harmful. His immune system is working to keep foreign proteins from getting in and causing allergic reactions. Early introduction to solids—before the system is ready—may predispose your child to allergies.

40.

"Who Do You Love More?"

If you are the parents of two or more children, you've no doubt heard them ask, "Who do you love more?" For a parent, this questions is almost always a shock to hear, mainly because you work so hard at giving equal amounts of love and attention to all of your children. There's really no way you can get through to your children that you love them both equally. The best you can do is treat them as equally as possible and love them all too much!

Love all of your kids unconditionally, for who they are. Help siblings to see that although they are different, they are loved and appreciated for the unique things that make them special. You can cut down on the frequency of the question, "Who do you love more?" by making sure to follow a few simple guidelines in your approach to raising your children.

Pay attention to your children equally. Teach them that it's okay to ask for attention and that attention comes in many forms. Your children should also be encouraged to pay some attention to their siblings.

Deal with your children's feelings. Instead of trying to avoid sibling rivalry, teach your children the importance of sharing and helping each other. Help them to express their feelings of jealousy and to control them with words instead of actions.

When your children learn to develop their own nurturing relationships with one another, they'll feel less competitive and less jealous of each other. Give your older children some responsibility for your younger children. Ask them to help younger siblings bandage small cuts or carry their toys to their rooms. Encourage your children to comfort and care for each other when one is hurt or sad. And whenever possible, give them a task that requires teamwork to complete. Cleaning their toys out of the family room or setting the table will help them learn the value of working together.

The most important thing to remember when dealing with sibling rivalry is never to compare your children. Comparisons among siblings create a competitive atmosphere. Treat them as equals—even when disciplining them. When they experience the same consequence at the same time and for the same duration, neither can conclude that one is more important than the other.

By reducing sibling rivalry, we help our kids focus on navigating life's challenges without worrying about measuring themselves against others. Decreasing sibling rivalry means valuing each child separately from and independently of the other, and encouraging without comparing.

41.

Choose Your Words Wisely

As tempting as it may be to tell your children who are rambunctious at the supermarket, "If you don't stop, I'm going to leave you here," it's important to understand that statements such as this, though unintentional, have a huge negative impact on our children. The words you use to communicate with are critically important to the self-esteem, emotional health, and personal empowerment of our children. Words can empower—and words can diminish. Words can nurture or shame, encourage or scold. You have to be careful which words you use when attempting to control your children, because they can be harmful and damaging to their spirits.

Young children's worst fear is that they will get lost or be left alone. Threatening children by playing into their fears of abandonment is not wise. Though you may be feeling exasperated and angry at your children's behavior, don't lose control. Take a breather, and come up with a solution to end bad behavior. Then choose your words wisely when presenting it.

There are many phrases parents often blurt out unintentionally that can be just as damaging as the one above. Learn what they are in order to avoid using them in the heat of the moment.

"We never wanted children!" or something to this effect is an inexcusable phrase in parenting. Regardless of what your children have done, and no matter what tone of voice you use, this type of response is completely inappropriate. If you find yourself constantly feeling this way or thinking these thoughts, get some professional help.

"You ought to be ashamed of yourself!" This will give your children overwhelming feelings of guilt. The belief is that if the children are shamed into feeling guilty, they'll stop their behavior. The bad behavior may stop, but these words will still fill your children with feelings of guilt and shame. Ask yourself if that is your true intention for your children.

"Why can't you be more like your sibling?" Say this to your children, and you're not only contributing to sibling rivalry—you're instigating it. When you compare your children, one will always end up as the one who is not smart enough or not good enough.

"Let me do that for you—you're taking too long!" Taking over and doing things for children that they can do themselves makes them feel unimportant and useless. We all fall into this scenario from time to time because we're always harried and looking to save time. But you're making more work for yourself in the long run if you're constantly doing for your children now. Your children will come to expect that you will always be there to take care of things. This will stunt their own maturity and limit their capabilities.

So maybe you've said one or more of these phrases to your children in the past. That doesn't mean you are an abusive or cruel parent. But you are guilty of using language in a negative way, which could lead to emotional damage. By becoming aware of certain phrases and their negative implications, you can refrain from using them in the future. Children are resilient. They will respond to your cues. Find other words to use instead, and the things you say will have a powerful, positive effect on your children.

42.

Family Game Night

Having a regular "family game night"—whether once a week or once a month—is the perfect way to build family unity. It's something you can start when your children are little, and continue on until they are well into their teens. True, with teens you may find a little resistance, but if you are determined to make it work for your family, insist that attending family game night be a family rule with no possible exceptions.

Make this night special by setting it apart from all others. It should be a night where TV, phone calls, work—even video games—are forbidden. The children may still resist. Once they see how much fun it can be, they'll get into the idea and begin to look forward to game night.

Each game night, a different family member should pick the game for that evening, and another should choose and prepare the snack. If you have young children, include them in both selecting the game and preparing the snack. Give that resistant teen the job of picking the game for the first time.

Remember—the purpose of family game night is to create quality family time that doesn't revolve around discussing problems, schoolwork, or punishment. It's a time for fun and fun alone. Try changing the location of the night every so often—maybe take the family out for miniature golf or to a movie instead—as long as it's on the night selected. Most bookstore cafes even let people hang out and play games at their tables, if you're looking for a little change of scenery. Keep in mind that ultimately it doesn't matter what you do, when you do it, or where you do it—just as long as you're doing it together!

43.

Surviving the Family Vacation

When you have kids, your family trip can't really be called a "vacation" anymore—it should be referred to as a family "relocation." You're performing the same tasks from your everyday life—feeding the kids and keeping them occupied and out of trouble—with only a change of scenery to call it a vacation. Can you survive a week away from home with your kids?

The answer is yes; you can, but when planning a vacation away with young children, be realistic. Pick vacation spots that are kid-friendly to make the experience as enjoyable as possible. Be aware that you're going to be bogged down with suitcases. The amount of paraphernalia you'll need to bring for your kids can be overwhelming. Extra diapers, blankies, stuffed animals—whatever they need to make them feel at home while they're away from it.

Don't go to someplace like Europe without making sure there are more than enough activities to keep your children occupied. Seven days of touring Paris offers nothing remotely exciting for a toddler. If you must visit such a place with young children, do loads of research first. Find the best playgrounds Paris has to offer, and get a list of the city's best children's museums. Skip the Louvre on this trip, and spend a day picnicking at Versailles instead.

When your kids are older, you can get as close to a real vacation as possible, provided you plan for their entertainment, in addition to your own. While an eleven-year-old doesn't need to be entertained by you every second, she still needs to keep busy. Let her choose books to bring along. This is also the perfect time to allow your child unlimited access to a portable video game. Allow her to play and read as much as she wants whenever you're traveling. This is her vacation, too—a time for easy reading and mindless play.

No matter what their ages, your kids need a lot of opportunities while on vacation to run around and get rid of excess physical energy. Try to walk as much as possible—sightseeing or just hiking—and visit playgrounds whenever possible. Schedule a lot of free time for these activities. You'll feel less rushed, and your kids will feel like you're doing some things just for them.

On your family vacation, it helps to remember that your eleven-year-old is still a child. She's going to get hungry, tired, or bored, and you'll have to limit your expectations. She may not be able to walk up to the top of the Statue of Liberty or make it through the entire Air and Space Museum. So be flexible and take your child's complaints seriously. You and your spouse may want to split up once in a while and find alternate ways to accommodate everyone in the family. Keep sightseeing short and sweet. It helps to make the cultural aspect of your vacation more interesting for them by researching the sights that you'll visit before your trip. Go online or to the library, and give your kids a preview of what they'll be seeing. This can create excitement and enthusiasm for your children, and they'll find fewer things boring.

The best way to make the most out of your family vacation is to be prepared and to be flexible. Keep in mind that if your kids are happy and stimulated during your travels, you can relax and have a good time!

44.

Always Be Polite!

The key to teaching children about respect boils down to the example you set. If children are treated with respect, they will learn what it means to respect others. If children are spoken to politely, those children will learn to speak politely to others.

It's best to begin building the foundation for mutual respect early on. Although young children don't truly understand the behavior expected of them, by the time they are three, they generally know right from wrong, and they are aware that their behavior can affect other people. That's why it's important to ready your child for social interaction from the very beginning.

First, you need to define for your children words such as "respect," "manners," and "courtesy." One way is to explain to them that manners are like rules. Young children respond well to the sanctity of rules. They know that if they want to play baseball, for instance, they need to learn the rules. If they want to play a board game with friends, they first must learn the rules. Apply this to teaching your children manners. Explain to them that people need certain rules to help them know how to act with each other. Some of these rules have to do with being polite and respectful—saying "please" and "thank you." Some have to do with respecting others' feelings—refraining from use of words and phrases like "stupid" or "shut up." Some rules include addressing adults as "Mr." and "Mrs." and treating them with respect. When you reprimand your kids consistently from an early age and reinforce these rules, they begin to see this pattern. Paying respect and extending proper courtesy becomes automatic.

Explained in easy enough terms, the patterns of social conduct will eventually become clear to your child. As kids get older, their communication becomes more sophisticated, but with constant reinforcement, these basic courtesies will become second nature.

Despite your best efforts, keep in mind that kids will be kids. Your teenager will still talk back to you, and your five-year-old may call an adult "Fat Butt," despite your repeated attempts at setting examples of respect and politeness. Before you die of embarrassment or punish your kids for the rest of their lives, remember that everybody slips from time to time. If your children are successfully taught the ways of mutual respect, it will be easier for them to get back on track after a slip-up. With your love and understanding, they can ultimately learn to respect others and function politely in society.

45.

"I Didn't Do It"

You're standing over an overturned bowl of cereal and a puddle of milk in the center of your carpet and looking into the guilty faces of your three children. "Who spilled the cereal?" you ask.

None of them will admit anything to you. "It wasn't me," they say.

But unable to hold it in any longer, your youngest finally lets the cat out of the bag and incriminates your oldest. The oldest looks down guiltily.

How do you cope with your little liar? How do you make him understand that you expect the truth from him all the time—no exceptions? Children fear being punished as a result of their misbehavior. They are scared to tell the truth if it means they'll be punished or have a privilege taken away. But they need to be taught that lies—little or big—have enormous consequences. Such consequences don't have anything to do with being punished, but they have a lot to do with honesty and trust.

Teach your children that you value honesty. Encourage them to be honest, and make sure they know that even if they do something wrong, you can work it out together.

Don't focus on the lie itself—for instance, in the scenario above, let your child know that you understand it was an accident and that accidents happen. Focus more on cleaning up the mess, rather than on who made it. Reinforce to him that even mommy spills things and sometimes makes mistakes. That way, he may not be so afraid to tell you the truth the next time. Enlist his help in cleaning up the spill, and try injecting a little humor into the situation to defuse the moment. It may help to ease your child into admitting his responsibility.

Try not to overreact, no matter the damage! So maybe the carpet was expensive, and maybe the milk stain will never completely come out. But if you make too big a deal over it in front of your child, he'll become too scared to tell you the truth. Let him know that you know he's guilty, and remind him in a firm yet gentle voice that he shouldn't lie. "Your brother and sister saw you spill your cereal—please don't lie again in the future."

Reprimand your child, and explain to him that lying is not acceptable behavior. You may have to resort to punishment or taking away a privilege, but be sure that the degree of punishment fits the degree of the lie. If your children understand that there are consequences to lying, they may think twice about lying again.

Most importantly, when trying to teach your children the value of honesty, never get caught in a lie yourself! Everyone is guilty of a little white lie here and there, so watch what you say in front of your kids. At preschool, don't tell another parent who called the night before that you couldn't take the call because you were in the shower if your four-year-old is standing right there and knows perfectly well you were watching television. That's sending mixed messages.

Honesty builds trust. You want your children to understand the importance of trust. You need to trust them, and they need to trust you—at all times. Explain that lying about something small—like spilling milk—isn't so horrible because of the mess, but because of the lie. Tell them that the next time, if they tell you the truth—no matter what—you'll promise not to punish them.

46.

It's All in a Day's Work

With all the stress that comes with having a new baby—or having another baby—it's easy to get caught up in a daily whirlwind of working, running, doing, and scheduling without finding time to take five and breathe. Sometimes the stress is unbearable; you can't keep up. You love your kids dearly—but you wish they weren't so needy.

Working parents often feel so guilty about being away from home that they try to make up for it by "doing it all" when they come home. But as most stay-at-home parents can tell you, the job of caring for your kids isn't part-time, it's full-time, and it's impossible to fit a full-time job into an evening. If you work nine to five, tips and advice on "doing it all" are going to be useless. If you can afford it, you and your spouse may want to rethink your working status.

Couples cringe at making this decision—and it's understandable. Both partners have worked long and hard at building their careers, and neither may be in the position to put theirs on hold—not to mention the financial benefits of having two incomes. After all, raising kids can be costly. But it's important to be honest with yourselves. Is your family functioning properly in its current status? Are your children happy? Are you taking home enough extra money—after paying for child care—to really make a difference in your family's quality of life?

It's not an easy decision, by any means. But if you're finding yourselves dissatisfied with the amount of time you have with your children and you have some flexibility with your work, it's time for some big changes. No one will think less of you if you leave your job to stay home with your children or if you only work part-time. In fact, most people support that decision. Maybe it's time to tighten the belt, stick to the bare necessities for you and your kids, and make a change. Weigh all the pros and cons of you or your spouse leaving work. Which of you earns more? Which of you works closer to home? Which of your employers might allow you to work three days a week?

Chances are that you'll all be happier with this new decision. Your energy levels will skyrocket, and you'll wonder how you ever chose to work away from home or full-time in the first place. Sure, you'll have to cut back on a few luxuries, but what's a new dishwasher or a new pair of shoes compared to the extra time you have for your children?

47.

Act, Don't React,
to Your Child's Misbehavior

The next time that your child cries or throws a tantrum, look at it from this perspective: He is really acting out to get attention. It's easy to get caught up in the drama and start looking for ways to make your kid stop—but what you should do is find a seat in the audience and wait for the performance to end!

Parents of misbehaving children need to understand what's behind the behavior, and most importantly, to learn not to take it personally. We often take our children's actions personally and react by screaming, arguing, or handing out punishments.

Instead of reacting to your children's misbehavior, the experts say to act. Give positive guidance. Build your children's confidence by communicating with them, and help them learn to resolve conflicts and problems independently.

As a parent who wants to keep the peace, it's always tempting to step in and mediate when there's a conflict. Your kids are fighting in another room, and one emerges in tears. After making sure that neither of them has been physically hurt, resolve to stay out of it! Don't get caught up in the drama of it all. Instead, calmly tell your children, "I didn't see what happened, so it doesn't make sense for me to take sides. Go into your room, and work it out for yourselves."

By using natural and logical consequences as an alternative to threats and punishments, parents can begin to put their children's misbehavior in perspective. It isn't an easy approach, but once you get in the habit of practicing this form of discipline, your children will stop acting out (since you won't be calling attention to it) and learn to work out their problems on their own.

48.

Baby Bootie Camp

When your new baby turns one month old, celebrate! You've survived. The first month home with a newborn can be very much like baby boot camp, where your mental and physical endurance will be pushed to the limits. If you've just begun your thirty-day reserve stay at Baby Bootie Camp, here are a few tips to help ease you into the second month.

Change your answering machine message. As soon as you arrive home from the hospital with your newborn, change your message to let all your callers know the important information: the baby's name, time of birth, weight, and when you'll be able to get back to them. Then let the machine answer your calls for a few days.

Prepare meals in advance, or keep take-out menus handy. You are trying to make the first month home with your baby as free from stress as possible. You'll have to relinquish some responsibility from time to time, and taking off your chef's hat is an easy way to do so.

Hire a person to clean your house. If you've always been the one to take care of the housework, this is the time to let someone else do it. Your new baby is going to take up most, if not all, of your time, and housework can fast become overwhelming. If money is tight, ask your mother, your spouse's mother, or a good friend to help with the straightening up.

When someone offers to help, take it! Whether it's to do laundry or go to the drugstore, now's not the time to be shy about accepting help. Everyone is always eager to help a new parent. Don't be afraid to ask.

Go electronic! Post the news of your baby's birth on a web site. Friends can see video footage, leave you messages, and in some instances, purchase gifts for your baby—all at the site. You can also apply for the baby's Social Security number on the Internet, order baby supplies, and pay bills, saving you the hassle of leaving the house.

Create a baby station in your kitchen. Dedicate a separate cabinet to bottles and bottle paraphernalia, formula, bibs, cloth diapers, and extra pacifiers. Make sure this area of the kitchen is well-lit at night—you'll be sleepy and disoriented at three in the morning, and you'll need to find everything easily.

Try not to get agitated with your spouse! Your spouse is a valuable asset during the first month home with a baby—so do your best not to alienate your partner or you'll be outnumbered. You'll be waking up at all hours of the night, which can lead to snapping and arguing. Remember to think about how much help your spouse is providing every day. You couldn't get through the day without that help, and you are grateful for it. Eventually, that irritating snore while the baby is screaming her head off won't seem so horrible.

49.

Raising Smart Kids

The facts are in—parents are the most important and valuable influences on their children's grades. It's not the amount of money you have, the education you have, which teacher your child has, or even the number of computers you have at home. It's what you do in the course of your normal, everyday family life to encourage your child's learning and understanding of the world that makes all the difference! It helps to know that there are many simple activities you can add to the time you spend with your child—fun, everyday activities that can make the most of their learning opportunities.

Believe it or not, a simple trip to the grocery store can provide a wealth of learning opportunities for your child. The produce department offers an opportunity to learn weights and measures. Using coupons offers the chance to better basic math skills. Comparison shopping can help even your youngest child learn the value of money.

Your trip to the supermarket also provides a good opportunity to teach your children about compassion. Demonstrate how money is needed to buy the basic necessities of life, and that many people in our country don't have enough money for all of them. Perhaps you can purchase a few extra canned goods and donate them to a local food drop after you leave the store. Some supermarkets collect food for the needy right at the register.

Your local library also presents an excellent opportunity for expanding your child's learning experiences. It's important to challenge your children during library visits, steering them toward fun research activities that they wouldn't find on their own. For instance, look for a book that lists the birthdays of famous people. Find a famous person who shares your child's birthday, and then help your child learn more about that famous person.

When you're alone with your kids in the car, play word games with them. This helps them develop their language skills. Play "Twenty Questions," or the ever-popular license plate game. Have a passenger grab a pencil and paper, and challenge your kids to come up with palindromes, rhymes, homonyms, or anagrams.

The goal here isn't just for your children to get good grades, but rather to help them become better thinkers overall. You can cover math, history, geography, and language—all in a day spent with your children. If you are subtle enough, your kids will never even know that they spent the day learning!

50.

When Super-Mom Feels
Less Than Super

The moment you've waited nine months for is finally here—the baby you've dreamed about is now a reality. Everything is great—except for the fact that you feel more miserable and more scared than ever. Welcome to postpartum depression (PPD).

PPD is very common, affecting more than half of all new mothers. It usually strikes during the first few days after giving birth, and can last sometimes for weeks. Symptoms include crying easily, feeling a sadness that's hard to shake, and an inability to concentrate. Doctors attribute PPD to a drop in hormone levels after birth combined with a lack of sleep. It's important to inform your doctor if you're experiencing symptoms of PPD, especially if they last for longer than a few weeks—the faster you get help to combat these "baby blues," the faster you can get back to enjoying your baby.

PPD aside, many women experience negative feelings after giving birth. Feelings of resentment toward your baby, worrying why you haven't fallen in love with your baby yet, feeling trapped, and feeling like you can't get anything done are all very common thoughts and emotions. You'll feel better if you share your feelings with your husband, your parents, and your friends.

You *will* fall in love with your baby. Caring for your child day after day establishes a bond that cannot be broken. By the time your baby smiles for the first time, you'll be under his spell.

Giving yourself some time alone, away from your baby, can do a world of good. If you're spending every waking moment with your baby, you need a break! Go out for lunch with a friend, take a long walk, or go shopping. Enlist a relative to watch the baby, and just get out. You'll feel better in no time, and chances are that you'll actually miss the baby you couldn't wait to leave two hours earlier.

All new mothers feel as if they can't get anything done. Newborns don't have a schedule—they cry for every reason, they eat when they're hungry, and they wet their clothes at the most inopportune times. It's hard for a new mom to gain momentum and complete even the smallest of tasks, such as taking out the trash or refilling the diaper bag. Slow down, and accomplish what you can. Things will eventually settle down a bit—just stop expecting too much of yourself.

New moms aren't supposed to do much beyond the basic tasks of the day. They cook, clean, change diapers, feed, bathe, and do laundry. Relax into the nurturing routine you create for you and your newborn. It's only here for a short time, and once it's gone, you're going to remember it as one of the best times of your life.

51.

Raising Friendly Kids

There are many ways you can help your kids feel more capable in social situations. But you must also realize that your children are born with certain personality traits and characteristics. If your children lean toward shyness, they may always experience some amount of social discomfort.

Shy children are likely to be more introverted and learn by listening and thinking about things. It's important to realize that this isn't a bad quality. Those who are extroverted learn by talking, and can be challenged by children who are quiet. But if you're determined to help your shy child open up, you should look for opportunities to demonstrate certain social behaviors to your children.

For example, if you are going to spend a weekend away at the home of friends who you haven't seen in years, you might talk to your child about the friends you are visiting and your connection to them. The more information you provide your child with, the more comfortable she'll feel with your friends. Let her share any concerns or anxieties she may have over meeting them.

Help your children find new kinds of social groups that might be of interest to them. During adolescence, children seek identity through group associations. If your son has an interest in music, encourage him to join the band at school. If your daughter enjoys art, find an art class with kids her own age.

Your child may always be a quiet, reserved person, and there's nothing wrong with that, provided she doesn't develop rude behavior. (People in society often tend to mistake shyness for rudeness.) Try new ways to help your shy child develop self-esteem and expand socially.

52.

Controlling Tempers...Yours!

When you have children, you're going to become angry. It's a given. You love your children, and you will hate being so angry with them. Many parents want to control their children's behavior, but they lack the skills needed to encourage them to comply.

When a situation provokes your anger, get into the habit of dealing with it while still maintaining control of your feelings. Let's say your children's toys are all over the floor, and you've asked them repeatedly to clean them up. Instead of screaming at them again, tell them what you expect of them and take action: "Kids, your toys are all over the living room. The television goes off until they're all put away." Turn off the TV, and give them a chance. They're not going to jump at your command and begin cleaning, but keep your cool. When they see that you mean what you say, they'll clean up their toys.

Another recipe for anger is two bickering children and a parent on the telephone. Their fighting grows louder and louder, and you're ready to explode. Instead, express your feelings: "Kids, I'm on the telephone, and I can't hear the person I'm talking to. I'm going to finish my conversation in the other room—when I return, I hope you will have worked out your differences."

Some of the most anger-producing moments between parents and children happen when parents see that their kids are not listening to them. Most often, this is because your children are distracted by something else. This can be extremely infuriating, so make sure you have their undivided attention before giving them your request. If your son is doing his homework with the TV on and you remind him that he won't get good grades if he watches TV while doing homework, he may agree with you and mumble something under his breath. Did he hear what you said? No!

Instead, try asserting your values and expressing their importance. Tell him, "Homework is more important than TV. Turn it off until the homework is done." You may have to turn the television off yourself, but he'll get the picture, and you will have avoided feeling angry.

It's hard—but it's not impossible—to control your emotions when you're angry. The trick is to give yourself a small amount of time—breathing room—before you give in to your emotions. If you feel yourself becoming very angry with your children, control your desire to scream and yell. Walk into another room, or take a deep breath and count to ten. It will give you a chance to assess the situation and determine the proper way of dealing with it—minus the anger.

53.

Teaching Your Children Responsibility

Being responsible means acting wisely without being guided, told, pressured, or threatened into action. It's the ability to make decisions and be accountable for them. Our children learn to be responsible by feeding and dressing themselves, going to sleep on their own, playing independently, helping with simple chores, and behaving within the limits.

As they grow older, children become more and more capable of certain responsibilities. It's important to give your kids new responsibilities so that they'll have a greater sense of accomplishment. Children who are given responsibility for tasks that they are capable of performing are likely to have a greater sense of belonging in the family and feel as though they can contribute to life in a meaningful way. As a parent, you must be careful to have realistic expectations of what responsibilities your child can handle. Chores and tasks must be age-appropriate and fit their developmental level. Children can't do what they aren't capable of doing yet!

Remember that your kids will need help and constant reminders to accomplish most tasks. When you're instructing your children on how to complete a new task—such as putting dirty clothes in the hamper—be sure to break the task down into steps, and give them clear directions on how to complete them. If they know the directions, they're more apt to practice them on their own. Even if they can't complete a chore at first, kids are quick learners—they'll have it down pat in just a matter of months.

Children are too young to understand the importance of responsibilities such as keeping rooms clean and completing chores every week. So don't be surprised if your child doesn't develop a passion for setting the table. Also, while many children love learning new chores, once they become "old," the kids may lose interest.

Giving children tasks that are real and that help your family function may encourage your kids to do them more often. They will enjoy the sense of accomplishment that new responsibility brings them. Learning responsibility is a lifelong process that begins at home. Understand that kids' capacity for responsibility is incremental, and they must learn the skills necessary to become responsible people. With patience and guidance, they'll be mowing the lawn and vacuuming in no time!

54.

Kindergarten and
First-Day Jitters

Walking through new school doors on the first day of school can be pretty hard on kids of any age. Whether your child is going to preschool for the first time, entering kindergarten, or moving up to middle school, you need to help your kid get ready.

For a preschooler's first day, your main concern will be separation anxiety. It helps to begin the separation routine a few days before your child's actual first day. If possible, include your child's teacher or a carpooling partner in the routine. Illustrate the steps your child will take, from hanging up her belongings to what she will be doing after school. The key here is making sure that your preschooler is comfortable enough for you to leave.

The same ultimately goes for your child's first day of kindergarten. If she's been to a preschool program, the separation anxiety may not be so great—but it could still exist. If possible, familiarize your child with her new classroom and teacher. If your child is going to be riding on a bus, do a short practice walk to the bus stop. Point out landmarks, and discuss safety issues.

It's helpful for parents to establish an evening and morning schedule a week before school begins—and stick to it. Have your child help make up the schedule, and include bath time, bedtime, wake-up time, and lunch preparation. Help her pack her book bag for the next day, and explain what each item is for. Be sure to give her some responsibilities of her own.

Help to calm your child's nerves on the morning of the first day. Go over again what she can expect at school, and tell her that you can't wait to hear all about his day when she comes home. Make her favorite breakfast, and let her wear her favorite shirt. When the bus finally comes, leave your child with a positive attitude. Don't prolong your good-bye—make it short and sweet. Long good-byes can make children more nervous.

Older children have anxieties about the first day of school, as well. While they may act out differently—perhaps you'll notice a change in behavior the week before school starts—they need to prepare for their first day in a similar way. Establish a routine a few nights before in which your child goes to sleep earlier, make sure she's prepared with the proper school supplies, and let her know you are there for her should she have any questions or concerns.

Your child's first day of school can set the tone for the entire school year. That's why it's important to prepare for it, begin it calmly and easily, and ensure that your child is as comfortable as possible.

55.

Is There a Tattletale
in Your Midst?

Young children often get tattling and telling mixed up. Since tattling can be extremely irritating and set off a hysterical chain reaction among siblings or friends, we need to teach our children the difference between the two early on.

Tattling is what some children do to get others in trouble or to get attention. Telling is what some children do when someone needs help or is hurt. Tattling is never good, but telling is sometimes very important. Your child should always tell an adult when he is scared, is in danger, is uncomfortable about a situation, or needs protecting.

Ask your child for ideas about handling a tattletale. What would his response be if he saw a friend throw a toy in class? Offer suggestions as to what he can do instead of tattling: walk away, pick up the toy and put it back, or ask his friend not to throw toys. Explain to your child that it is really not his business—since it does not affect him and nobody was hurt by the toy, he should not let it bother him.

When two children are tattling on each other at a preschool play date, give them the choice of working it out and continuing to play together or playing separately. When the kids realize that you're not going to settle it for them, they will most likely choose to work it out and continue playing together.

Despite your greatest efforts, your kids will exert tattletale tendencies at some point in their young lives. The best you can do is tell them that you don't approve of the tattling, and that if they are really upset about the situation, they should come up with a creative solution.

56.

Keeping Your Kids Safe

Sooner or later, your children will ask for freedom to do more. It's important to allow your children the proper growth toward personal autonomy, but even more important to do so while also ensuring their safety and security.

Start small. Preschoolers can learn basic safety rules, but keep in mind that they become confused when learning how important it is that they do not speak to strangers. Parents first must explain to them what strangers are. Don't take it for granted that your four-year-old can spot a stranger. Teach your preschooler that a stranger can look like a regular man or woman, and that not all strangers are bad. But since we can't tell if people are nice or mean just by looking at them, it's a good idea not to talk to them unless they are with Mommy and Daddy.

By age ten or eleven, your kids are going to ask for a big leap in their freedom. Should you allow your ten-year-old to ride her bike to a friend's house? Possibly not. Statistically, a ten-year-old might be responsible enough to make a short trip safely. But only you know your child. Can you count on her to be responsible? Will she follow safety rules on her own? Do you trust that she will make proper judgments by herself? There is also the issue of your child being exposed to harmful strangers. It may be best not to let her completely out of your range at this age.

Before you let your teenagers out on their own, it's important to establish clear rules of safe behavior. Offer them hypothetical situations, and ask them to come up with solutions. Impress upon them the importance of communication—such as calling you when they arrive or before they leave to come home. If your child is going over to a friend's house, make sure he promises to call you if they change their plans or decide to go someplace else.

You can never predict how even the most responsible children will react in a compromising situation. All you can do is prepare them for what could happen, and teach them the basic concepts for dealing with potentially threatening situations. When they venture out of the house, they should always be aware of their surroundings and keep a safe distance from strangers. They should avoid isolated, unsupervised settings, and know that some strangers—policemen, store clerks—are good people to approach for help.

If you could, you'd never let them out of your sight. But that isn't being realistic. At a certain age, your children need to venture out into the world on their own, to develop their basic survival instincts, and learn how to take better care of themselves.

57.

Time with Grandparents

You may not always agree with them, and you may not always even like them, but your opinions of your own parents and your spouse's parents should have no bearing on your children's relationship with their grandparents. Grandparents provide a warm, nurturing environment for your children—even if they haven't been or aren't warm and nurturing to you. Most grandparents often correct the mistakes they made with their children by the time they get a chance to develop a relationship with their children's children.

Let your children go alone with their grandparents sometimes—it will give them the chance to get to know your kids better and form a loving, lasting relationship. With you out of the picture, they'll also get the chance to indulge your kids with all that's taboo at home—excess candy, toys, and ice cream! But don't get upset when this happens. They're only doing their job as grandparents.

If you're sending your kids for the day or for the weekend with their grandparents, be sure to pack a bag of things that they'll need.

Also remember to put children's car seats in their car, and teach them how to buckle your kids safely. Provide them with all your important phone numbers—just as you would for a baby-sitter.

Your parents or your spouse's parents will surprise you with the relationships they form with your children. You may learn things you never knew about them, hear stories you've never heard before, or be reminded of things you long ago forgot. Not all kids have grandparents. Be grateful if yours have theirs, and teach them to treasure every moment spent with them.

58.

Praise Versus Encouragement

Helping to build your children's self-esteem is an important part of raising kids. One way parents can go about building their children's self-esteem is to praise them often. But even praise must be given with clear and careful thought.

You need to determine the difference between praise and encouragement. Encouragement can be described as any kind of positive reinforcement you can offer your child. Praise is more complimentary. Try to be consistent in encouraging children, and save praise for times when they have made extra efforts to be successful. For example, say you've just praised your son's efforts for his book report. Give him encouragement, too: "That was a difficult book to read. I'm proud of you for sticking with it." You're not just praising the results of the accomplishment; you are also saying that he is a capable person.

It's easy to praise and encourage children when it comes to schoolwork, but parents need to extend positive attention into other areas of their children's lives. Show encouragement for your child's everyday tasks such as decorating his bedroom, playing sports, or interacting with friends and siblings. This shows him that you're proud of all his gifts, which helps build self-esteem.

Children should learn that they don't need to rely on others for validation of a job well-done. Teach your children to acknowledge their own successes. "Great job painting your bedroom! Give yourself a pat on the back!"

Praising too much can be a problem—especially with children who work hard and are eager to please. Be sure to give them an equal balance when you offer kind words to them. Praise them, yes, but encourage them, too!

59.

The Working Mother
Versus the Stay-at-Home Mom

While most working mothers are happy with their decision to go back to work, they often sense disapproval from mothers who have chosen to stay at home with their kids. If you find yourself caught up in this bitter battle, it's important to know the pressures mothers face on both sides of the fence. Most importantly, no woman should think that a decision different from hers is wrong.

No matter what employment decision a mother makes, she will feel pushed in another direction. All women are under enormous pressure when they become mothers: pressure that says a mother should spend all her time at home with her children, and financial pressure that forces a mother to go back to work, whether she wants to or not. In this atmosphere, even mothers who feel good about their decisions experience tension, hostility, and disapproval. Keep an open mind; just because your best friend decides to leave her law practice to stay at home and raise her children—a notion you can't imagine—it doesn't mean her decision wasn't the right one.

The stay-at-home mom's point of view is rooted in identity. She almost never gets the respect that she rightly deserves. She's falsely presumed to be boring, with no concerns or areas of interest other than those of her children. While she easily has the most mentally and physically challenging job there is, she's immediately labeled as "not working." Meanwhile, she may also feel guilty about giving up her career and being the one to stay home while her husband financially supports the family.

Working mothers experience tremendous guilt, too—especially about being away from home every day. They wonder if their kids are getting the care that they need from the nanny, baby-sitter, or preschool. They fear that their children will love their nanny more than their own mother. They miss a lot by being away—the baby's first steps and first words. They question their decision, wondering if they're being selfish for wanting a career.

It's essential for all mothers to accept the fact that there isn't one right choice for every family. Regardless of employment status, mothers today need each other. Whether it's a shoulder to lean on, or an offer to take the kids when you're in a bind, almost every mother—working away or at home—can provide you with support that you won't find anyplace else. So before you judge another mother for her decision to work or stay home, remember that all moms are in the same boat: They all want to nurture and care for their kids as they grow and spend quality time with them.

60.

When Dad Feels Undermined

When Dad works full-time and Mom is home with the children all day, it's easy for the kids to fall into the "Mommy" trap. Even though Dad is in the kitchen, the kids will still go find Mom to ask her to pour them some juice. It becomes almost automatic for them to ask Mommy for everything. However, this pattern can lead to a more problematic issue. It becomes routine for Mom to make decisions for the children, despite the fact that Dad may have already spoken. Eventually, Dad will feel angry and resentful that his spouse is constantly undermining him. Undermining ways can only be harmful.

When the kids ask for one more cookie, if Dad says no and Mom says it's okay, Dad feels less authoritative in front of his children. It doesn't matter that Mom knows the kids skipped their snack that day and are entitled to more cookies. If Dad says no, Mom should back him up. Then she can speak to him separately and explain her point of view to him.

You and your spouse may disagree about certain issues. You may not feel as if it's okay for your child to jump in puddles, but if your spouse has already agreed to it, let it go. Discuss the issue later when the kids aren't around. Children will quickly learn to play one parent off of another if they feel that one of you is leaning toward a certain reply.

Making child-rearing decisions that conflict with those of your spouse can cause problems. Parents should keep two things in mind: Respect each other, and always have the best interests of the children at heart!

61.

"I'm Sorry"

Parents are only human. We're going to make mistakes, behave less than perfectly, and sometimes hurt the ones we love—even our children. Fortunately, we can make amends and reverse our hurtful behavior by apologizing.

When you make mistakes or lose your temper, you can use the situation to set an example for your children by making an obvious apology and asking for forgiveness. Asking for forgiveness is an important part in the apology process, because it benefits both parties involved. Accepting an apology also shows that the person offering the apology is respected as a human being.

Empty apologies occur in the home frequently. Your older child punches the younger on the arm. You immediately instruct your older child to say that she's sorry, which she does, and the situation is over.

Fostering a more effective apology takes a little more work, but it is well worth the time and effort. The next time you're tempted to demand an apology, take your child aside and try to discover what motivated the behavior. Talk to her about what she did and how it affects the entire family. Advise her how to avoid lashing out at her sibling in the future. Finally, give her a chance to apologize sincerely. As role models for your children, the most effective way to illustrate the power of an apology is to teach by example. If you say something that's hurtful to your children or take your anger or frustrations out on them, make it a point to give them a sincere apology. Don't brush it off or make light of it. When your kids see that you take repentance seriously, they will, too.

62.

A Single Parent
Is Double the Parent

Nobody doubts that single parents have it rough. A single parent with custody of children must be both mother and father to those children and take on all the responsibilities that come with both of those roles. A single parent doesn't have the support of another adult when certain problems arise. But single parents can learn to function effectively minus those two extra hands and survive the trials and tribulations of parenthood.

Single parents, though heavily burdened with double the responsibilities of married couples, must find time for themselves. It's important to set aside a block of time each week that's just for you. Plan to do something you enjoy that brings you happiness. This should not be any activity that is an obligation. Take advantage of family and friends who offer to baby-sit your children. Trade off with other parents who also need time alone. If you have a cooperative ex, take turns providing each other with time off.

Single-parent support groups can be enjoyable and fulfilling. Joining such a group may not be something you are comfortable with, but attending a trial meeting may surprise you. It can be a relief to meet people in the same situation as you—with the same gripes, problems, and needs. More often than not, you'll share tips, learn coping strategies, and gain confidence in your parenting abilities.

If you're sharing custody of your children with your ex, try to keep the kids' lives as normal as possible. Work out living and custody arrangements that suit everyone's needs. Keep the items that go back and forth between houses to a minimum—it will be easier on you and your children if they have two of many things: sets of toys, clothes, and toiletries for both houses.

Most importantly, behave with civility and kindness when it comes to your ex. Remember, it is for the sake of your children, who are coping with this situation as best they can. This may not be possible in all situations, but if your issues don't involve abuse or absentee parents, getting along with your former spouse can make life less stressful for everyone involved. It will please your children to see their parents treating each other with respect.

Finally, if your child wants to spend the weekend with your former spouse, even though it's technically your weekend, give in. It doesn't mean he loves you less or wants to live with your ex. He just has a need to be there this weekend. Respect that. Feeling anxiety over such things will eventually escalate into a scenario containing lawyers, custody battles, and stress.

63.

Grateful Children

Teaching our children to be grateful requires parents to practice gratitude. We must remember to give thanks verbally for all that we have instead of constantly complaining about all that we lack.

Gratitude is often practiced in most homes at bedtime or around the dinner table. Parents ask their children to name three things they are grateful for. For children who have had a lousy day or are dealing with their own, private problems, it's a refreshing exercise to be able to find things to give thanks for when life seems so bleak.

You can teach your children to be grateful on a daily basis by reminding them to say thank you. Many children think it is proper to say thank you only when they receive something, but children should also be taught to appreciate the kind actions of another person. If your neighbors help your son retrieve his ball from their yard, instruct your son to say thank you. If your daughter gets a ride home from a friend's parent, remind her to be gracious.

Don't let Thanksgiving be the only time your family expresses gratitude. Gratitude can help heal a family's woes and foster its growth if it is addressed often. Go out of your way to give your children opportunities to feel grateful at least once a month. Volunteer at a local soup kitchen or collect toys for homeless children. Visit a children's hospital or a nursing home. Your kids will not only feel a sense of gratitude for the fortune in their own lives; they'll develop a sense of compassion for those less fortunate.

64.

DEAR Time:
Drop Everything And Read!

It's no secret that reading aloud to your child is the single most important factor in turning your child into a reader. Fifteen-plus minutes of reading to your children daily is the most effective method of reading instruction. Reading also increases their awareness levels, exposes them to different people and cultures, sparks their interests in various topics, and boosts their imaginations.

When you read to your children, read books that you both enjoy. Vary the selection of books you read to them, and offer them stories that focus on a variety of topics. Try a fairy tale one night and a silly book the next. Even very young children can enjoy nonfiction and biographies.

If your daughter has selected the same book for several nights in a row, try not to show annoyance at reading it again. Instead, offer a new take by introducing another character or changing the ending.

Ask her to draw a picture from the story or make puppets to help act out the story. If you just can't bring yourself to read the book again, hide it and replace it with another that you think she'll like!

At the library, you can also expose your child to literature by borrowing books recorded on cassette tapes. The library also provides storybooks on CD-ROM, which bring many classic children's stories to life on your computer.

Once your children have been bitten by the reading bug, look out! They'll want to read everything that they can get their hands on. Don't despair if your kids only want to read comic books or chapter books about Scooby-Doo. Let them read whatever age-appropriate books appeal to them. They'll branch out at their own pace. Just remember to give them your approval and encouragement.

65.

You Are Getting Sleepy....

Getting your infant to "sleep through the night" means different things to different people. Some new parents wish their baby would just wake twice a night for feedings, instead of three times. Others wish their baby would sleep until morning without waking. For the parents of newborns, the problem is not the amount of time their baby sleeps, it's how many times they're getting up at night. The challenge new parents face is getting their child to conform to a consistent sleep pattern.

Parents often fail to realize that they wake during the night, too. They adjust their positions, get up for the bathroom or a drink of water, or wake to a sudden noise. The key difference is that adults have learned to put themselves back to sleep. Infants must learn to master this, too—without the help of parents!

No parents like to hear their baby cry. They rush to comfort the baby with a bottle, a pacifier, or a soft blanket. After all, that's their job. They will do anything to get the baby to just stop crying!

But think of it this way: When your baby is crying in the middle of the night, maybe he's adjusting his position. Maybe he heard a noise. If you're rushing in to rectify the problem every time, you're not giving him the chance to fall back asleep on his own. As he grows older, he'll always expect to be rocked, fed, or patted, and you will be caught in an exhausting and debilitating pattern.

If your baby is not sleeping for longer lengths of time by the time he's three months old, consider making a few changes to your bedtime ritual. Try putting your baby to bed while he is still awake. You never go to bed when you're already sleeping. You go to sleep after you get into bed. Infants need to learn that, too.

Make the transitions easy for the baby. Spend some quiet time with him after you put him in the crib. Children associate bedtime with separation from you, and you don't want this time to be traumatic. Give him a special bedtime toy that he'll learn to associate with going to sleep. It can be a pacifier, a blanket, or a stuffed animal.

There are many sleep experts who differ on what to do if your infant still isn't sleeping through the night by five months old. Some say to let your baby "cry it out," though other experts don't support that theory. Parents who find themselves desperate for sleep—their baby's and theirs—should read up on what all the experts have to say on the subject and then decide what's best for their family. Keep in mind that the hours you spend modifying your baby's sleep patterns will translate into hours of blissful sleep for you and your baby. And extra sleep means happier, more energetic parents!

66.
The Perfect Play Date Myth

You and your sibling both have beautiful, bright-eyed two-year-olds. So what happens when, despite your good intentions, the kids just can't seem to get along? When, after 15 minutes into a play date, they're grabbing toys from each other's hands and pounding each other mercilessly? You and your sibling spend the entire time breaking up fights and comforting crying kids.

Play dates with other children who have sharing issues can be disastrous if arranged at either child's home. Neither child can bear to see the other playing with her toys. When this is the case, you can do one of two things. You can wait it out maybe three months or so—when your child has become a slightly better sharer or has passed through the phases of the problematic issues. Give it another try. This will also give your child a chance to miss her friend and forget about the previous disastrous play dates.

Another idea is to move play dates to locations outside the house, where your children won't be expected to share anything.

You can meet at indoor playgrounds, the nearest children's museum, or in the gym at the local community center. Pick any place where your children can enjoy each other's company and won't see others as threats to their toys.

Play dates can be wonderful experiences for children. They allow them the chance to interact with kids their own age and learn social skills like sharing. But remember to consider the personalities of all children involved when you're planning a play date, and tailor your play (and the location) to suit everybody!

67.

Find the Humor

The moment may come when you least expect it. You're fumbling through the kitchen, preparing a bottle for your baby at four in the morning, and snapping at your equally sleepy spouse for not leaving the clean nipples where you could find them. You fill the bottle, push past your spouse, head for your screaming baby, then promptly lean over the crib to give the child a bottle . . . of soda.

Luckily, you notice just in time (much to your baby's unhappiness) and grumpily head back to the kitchen. There, when you're even angrier, sleepier, and more frustrated, you hold up the baby bottle for your spouse to see. You're about to blame your spouse (for keeping the soda next to the formula in the fridge), but suddenly you're struck by the absurdity of it all. You laugh, your spouse begins to laugh, and both of you double over in a sleep-deprived fit of giggles in the kitchen while your baby continues to howl in the next room.

Try to find some humor in every situation, and make it a

priority to laugh over it every single day. You could let the daily frustrations and complications of a new baby aggravate you, anger you, and frustrate you, but that accomplishes absolutely nothing. Plus your baby is sure to sense your negative feelings and become more upset.

It's good to try to laugh some things off. Laugh at your forgetfulness, at your mistakes, at your stupidity, and at your confusion. Laugh when you leave your keys in the stroller or when you put a dirty diaper in the fridge. You'll feel better, your baby will feel better, and you'll have funny stories to tell when your child is older. Best of all, you may not make the same mistakes again.

68.

Getting Out of the House

Every new parent has experienced the confusion and the chaos of packing up a baby for an outing. How do you remember all that you need for an afternoon at the park? Diapers, wipes, extra bottles, extra clothes—why does an infant need so much stuff for an hour out of the house? you wonder. What could possibly happen if you got caught at the park without, say, a diaper cloth? Well, until it happens, you can never begin to understand the importance of being prepared for any baby emergency.

It only takes once. It may be that your son goes off his schedule and starts screaming for a bottle about two hours early. Suddenly the fifteen-minute walk home seems like hours, your baby's crying, and you're working up a sweat just waiting for the light to change.

Luckily, your baby won't suffer as much as you will. And you've learned a valuable lesson: the importance of keeping a checklist next to your diaper bag at all times. Next time, you can be sure that you won't forget the extra bottle—or anything else, for that matter!

69.

Alone Time

When you're the parent of a very active child, you often find that you have no time for yourself. But sometimes just a ten-minute period is all the time you need to regroup.

Try to spend a part of your day just with your child. Share a snack together, play a game, read, or exercise. Explain that this is your fifteen minutes of "together time." Don't let the telephone interrupt your together time, and don't use this time to make shopping lists or fold clothes.

When your child has had this together time, tell her that now it's time for each of you to have fifteen minutes of "alone time." Explain that this is the same amount of time as before, only you won't be together. Help her decide what to do during her fifteen minutes. She can listen to music, watch a video, color, or look at books—just as long as it's something that she can manage without you.

For the first few days, retreat to your bedroom. Close the door and stay inside, even if your daughter pleads with you to come out. Keep a clock close by, and reassure her every few minutes that you'll be finished with your alone time soon. Tell her, "I'll be out in (however many) minutes." After a few days of this, she should begin to get used to spending this fifteen minutes away from you.

You can use this alone time tradeoff throughout the day—while you're preparing dinner or cleaning up afterward, if you need to make an important phone call, or any time that you especially need a breather. Don't let guilt keep you from creating some time for yourself. You deserve this fifteen minutes alone, and your child benefits, as well, by learning to play independently.

70.

Have Your Baby Call My Baby!

It's beneficial to expose children under the age of two to other babies. Interaction with other babies sets the tone for friendships that follow. By the time they turn three, your children can begin to develop their own friendships.

First friendships may develop in daycare, in preschool, or through play dates arranged by you. In these settings, children learn skills such as taking turns, choosing games, and social diplomacy. Your child will also learn about unfriendly behavior. Use such circumstances to show your child how people should not treat their friends and teach about the importance of forgiveness.

Some children make friends easily, while others find making friends more difficult. Children need to be given good examples of how to be a good friend and treat a friend. When they see parents or older siblings relating to their friends, it gives them a better idea of how they can make and keep friends.

Hosting a play group at your home is a great way to

demonstrate to your child how friends should be valued. By opening your home, you're showing your child that you are comfortable and happy around other people and that he can be, too. Encourage your child to help you prepare lunch and a snack or set up his toys for sharing. Let him know exactly who will be coming to play and which activities you'll be doing. Have your child welcome guests into the house when they arrive and give them a tour of his room and play areas.

You've set the stage for comfortable play, and you've encouraged your child to be courteous, fair, and kind to his friends. This is the best that you can do—now you just have to sit back and watch your child's friendships blossom!

71.

Teach Good Judgment

Good judgment—recognizing when to say no, when a situation is dangerous, or when something is morally wrong—doesn't come naturally to children. Teaching your children how to make good decisions on their own is very valuable and important.

We can't anticipate all of the decisions that our children will face. What if your child's friend says to coat the bedroom wall with toothpaste? The child may think, "Well, Mommy and Daddy never said I *shouldn't* put toothpaste on my wall." More seriously, what if your child's friend wants to show off a parent's gun? Most parents think that this sort of occurrence happens mainly with older children, so they make sure to teach their preteen kids about the dangers of guns. But what if it happens on your five-year-old's play date?

Begin establishing rules when children are little—as young as two. As they get older, explain the rationale behind those rules. One way to teach good judgment is to let your children make a lot of their own decisions. If their choices are not life-threatening or unhealthy, let them experience the consequences of their mistakes—as painful or uncomfortable as they may be. If your thirteen-year-old daughter insists on wearing a tank top under her coat to school in February, let her. When she gets cold, she'll have learned not to wear a sleeveless shirt in the winter.

Giving children reasonable choices early on helps them learn to evaluate their decisions. Judgment skills learned in childhood should carry over into teen years, when they face even tougher decisions. When your teenager makes good decisions, you'll be glad that you spent the time to teach sound judgment.

72.

Getting Your
Toddler to Listen

Your two-year-old son is a sweet, good-natured little boy who is driving his parents crazy. He repeatedly ignores you and your spouse every time you call on him or ask him to do something.

Before you race to have his hearing checked, understand that this is very typical behavior for a two-year-old. It's referred to as "noncompliance," and it can be the most irritating and aggravating stage of development your child passes through.

Your son is testing you when he ignores you. He's testing to see if you'll back up your words with actions. That's why it's essential that you carry out your response if he chooses to ignore you. For instance, if you call him indoors for naptime and he doesn't come, go outside and physically bring him in. Once you start moving toward him to respond to your requests, he'll begin to realize that you mean business.

If this method of parental response doesn't work, you may have to investigate whether or not your son hears and understands you. Ask your pediatrician to check that his hearing and language skills are on target for his age. Checking his hearing is an easy process that your pediatrician can perform in the office. Checking his language is a bit trickier.

At age two, a child should be able to put two words together and form a short sentence. He should also have an extensive vocabulary of words, even if he chooses not to use them all the time. Test him with simple commands to see if he understands your requests. Tell him, "Please bring me your toy." Does he? If you ask him, "Where are your shoes?" can he tell you where they are? Most pediatricians can identify if there is a language or learning delay and can instruct you on what options you have. The key is to recognize the delays as early as possible. Early intervention can make the difference in overcoming the problem. You want your son to be brought up to speed before he begins kindergarten.

When your children are older and don't listen to you, there is still a reason for concern, though the root of the problem may be behavioral rather than developmental. If your three-year-old is defiant and refuses to listen, there are many different and appropriate methods of reversing the behavior. One common technique is the "1-2-3" method. When you ask your daughter to come to the table for dinner and she doesn't budge, refrain from asking her a second time. Instead, begin to count to three. If she doesn't follow your request by three, you then take her to her room. If she begins to throw a tantrum over being sent to her room, ignore it and keep her in her room for three minutes. After three minutes, ask her again to come to the table. If she refuses again, repeat the process.

It's important that no other communication takes place when practicing the 1-2-3 method—no yelling, screaming, or corporal punishment. This can be a safe and effective way of getting your little one to listen.

73.

Tall Tales from
Short People

Many kids tell tall tales—some with a flair that would make even a best-selling author seem boring. If your preschooler has developed a knack for fantasy, it just means that he is using his imagination to the fullest extent! But some children can spin some stories to the extreme. It's one thing if your child knows that his tales are just fantasy. It's another if he begins to believe them himself.

It's not unusual for a youngster to confuse the fine line between fact and fiction. Once a preschooler begins an account of something that happened to him, when the story picks up a momentum, it can grow to unbelievable proportions. The account may be something that actually happened to his older sibling, but in his three-year-old mind, it happened to him by association. Rarely is this a cause for concern. It's merely a standard development.

Older children tend to exaggerate, too, though they don't necessarily mean for their stories to grow out of control.

Exaggeration, children learn early on, is a great way to get grownups to listen.

The next time your child begins a tall tale, try reacting with minimal interest and little attention. Without an eager audience, your child's story will soon fade. Another approach to untruthful stories is to cut them off at the pass. When a farfetched fable has begun, say, "That's unbelievable. Sorry, but I don't listen to tall tales," or, "When you want to tell me something real that happened to you today, I'll listen to you!" If these approaches don't take the fantasy out of your child's stories, don't be too concerned. Either his knack for fiction will fade over time—or he'll become the next great publishing success!

74.

Having "The Talk"
with Your Kids

When the question is asked, "Where do babies come from?" how much information is too much information? The answer lies in the nature of your child's question. Parents need to understand exactly what their children are asking before they construct an appropriate answer.

For example, if your eight-year-old asks, "Mom, where did I come from?" make sure she's asking about reproduction before you begin a detailed description of the sperm and the egg. She may only really want to know in which city she was born. But assuming that your child really does want to know where babies come from, use this opportunity to convey your values about sexual activity and responsibility.

The concept of a seed growing inside a mother is something that most eight-year-olds can understand. Depending on the child and how the conversation is going, you can also include the father's involvement in planting that seed. The rule in discussing sex education is never to introduce a topic that hasn't yet crossed your child's mind. This is essential when talking about babies and conception with younger children. Experts suggest beginning every answer to a question about sex with, "Why are you asking?" That way, you can discover what's really on your child's mind, and address the question without raising too many more questions in the process.

When discussing sex education with your children, keep it short and simple. Answer their questions honestly, and use the correct terminology. If your child asks you a straightforward question, give a straightforward answer. If you are asked, "What's a virgin?" say, "A virgin is someone who has never had sex before." Your child may or may not ask you, "What is sex?" after that. If so, answer that, too. If not, table the discussion for now.

Your children won't grasp all of the concepts you talk about, but it's important that you try your best to satisfy their curiosity. Be absolutely sure to tell them that just because you and your spouse are comfortable talking to them about sex, others may not be. Tell them that you're glad they are coming to you with their questions, and it's a good idea to keep any further discussions about sex within the family. Recognize, too, that sex education is not a one-time talk that's over and done in fifteen minutes. The topic will surface again and again. It's the parents' job to seize the opportunities that come up in daily life to teach their children about sexuality.

75.

One-on-One Spouse Time

Working parents who are busy juggling careers and children never seem to have enough time for each other. Months can go by in the lives of a couple without providing a single opportunity for them to enjoy spending time together. But you can bring the romance back into your lives and return to the way that it was when you were a young couple first starting out. Go ahead and ask your spouse out on a date!

Some rules apply for married parents about to begin dating: A date is your commitment to spend time together relaxing and enjoying each other's company. A date does not include children or friends. And each spouse must take turns planning the dates. Think back to before you were married or had children. Remember the things you liked to do as a couple, and look for ways to recreate those experiences. Go to a concert or out for a night of dancing. Hit the driving range, watch a horse race, or go to the beach for a picnic on a nice night.

Many couples take dating one step further and incorporate it into their regular schedules. "Date nights" have become common among married couples—steady, set times to spend together without the children. A date night can be on any night of the week or the weekend (depending on your baby-sitter status), as long as you're consistent.

Couples who enjoy date nights regularly swear by them. It's easier to make it through a week of shuttling your kids around, preparing their meals, playing with them, and helping them with their homework when you know that your date night is there, a permanent fixture on your calendar!

76.

Cherish Your One and Only

One of the most common questions asked of young married couples is, "So when are you two going to have kids?" Often guests at the couple's wedding ask this question! Talk about pressure! The question—even if proposed by the dearest, well-meaning friends of the bride and groom—is a thoughtless, insensitive one.

Another inappropriate question is frequently asked of parents with one child: "So, when are you going to have another?" Is this really anyone else's business? The answer to this question may bring up feelings of sadness or embarrassment for the couple. We need to take into consideration how our questions might affect the feelings of these people. The fact is that it is entirely acceptable in this day and age for a well-rounded family to consist of two loving parents and one sweet, adorable child.

There are many families in this country with just one child. In fact, it is estimated that 41 percent of families in the United States have only one child. Whether having just one child was planned or destined, these parents may experience guilt feelings that are specific to this situation. They don't appreciate the added displeasure of having to answer to others.

The most common feeling these parents share is that they should have another child to give a playmate to the first one. They think that a sibling is the answer, but considering the number of siblings who don't get along, that isn't always the case. Friendship between siblings isn't a given! Child-rearing experts who study the effects of one-child families believe that only children develop exceptional social skills as a result of always being "the best" at home. That contributes to building the child's self-esteem, which in turn enhances development and the ability to get along with others.

One common misconception is that raising an only child is a snap, compared to raising two or three. Actually, the opposite is true. Parents of an only child invest everything they have into that one child, and everyone holds up the child's successes and failures to scrutiny.

Parents of an only child also fear that they are spoiling their child. Again, the experts disagree, pointing out that "spoiled" is a stage nearly all children pass through. In addition, if children are given everything they want whenever they want, they will be spoiled—whether there is one child or six children in the family!

77.

Double Your Fun!

Twins never cease to amaze everyone. Watch new parents push two infants around the mall one afternoon, and you'll see how many times they're stopped by strangers who wish them well, ask questions, or just "ooh!" and "ahh!" Watch these new parents for a bit longer, and you'll agree that raising twins requires boundless energy, patience, and enthusiasm.

New parents of twins need the same assistance as any new parents—only their needs are magnified. Twins often need to eat more frequently, thus interrupting their parents' sleep schedules more. Babies are likely to be on different schedules, and nursing moms of twins need double the rest so that they can produce more milk.

For new parents of twins, don't be shy about asking for help. Chances are that your friends and family members will be thrilled to watch your babies. Multiples have a certain power. They attract baby-lovers and charm even the most reluctant visitors. You shouldn't feel funny about asking your visitors to bring food, either! Frozen meals are the best for those many hectic days.

When twins are your second and third, it's important to pay a lot of attention to the older sibling. The oldest will probably feel ignored and left out when most visitors keep coming to gush over the new babies. Ask friends or family members to take the oldest out for a special day all his own.

There are many issues pertaining primarily to multiples that become more important as children grow. The worst thing that you can do is compare your twins or talk about them in their presence. Twins face questions from their friends and others every day that may lead them to feel as if they are two halves of one person instead of two individuals. Parents of multiples need to gently remind others that their children are individuals. Dress them differently and call them by their names rather than referring to them as "the twins."

Parents of toddler and preschool-age multiples sometimes complain that they are abandoned by friends who are uncomfortable with having so many kids over at one time. If you find yourself in this situation, let your friends know that it's okay to have just one of your kids over for a play date. This will actually serve two purposes—it'll be much easier for your friend and the kids, and it will afford you some special time alone with your other child.

Multiples are special, there's no question. Parents of multiples are special, too, and they earn a great deal of respect for what most parents of singles imagine is an impossible job. There's no question that the job is difficult, exhausting, and emotionally draining, but with two faces to look at and love each day, it's rewarding twice over!

78.

Time for Homework

A recent study on the effectiveness of homework proved some interesting facts. The study found that the academic benefits of doing homework seem to depend on a student's grade level. High school students who regularly completed their homework outperformed those who didn't. For middle school students, homework was only half as effective, and for elementary students, homework had no apparent impact on their achievements!

But improved grades and test scores are not the only reason that your child's teacher assigns homework. Homework helps students acquire self-discipline, organize their time, and recognize that learning can and should take place outside of the confines of school.

Many parents ask how much help they should be giving their children when it comes to homework. To answer that question, you need to think ahead to your ultimate goal. You want your children to be able to plan, manage, and execute their homework on their own. Obviously, if you do your children's homework for them every night, that's not helping them achieve that. If you keep doing your children's homework, they won't develop proper study skills.

Parents should focus on getting homework sessions to the point where their involvement is usually nothing more than looking over their children's shoulders without their knowing it. How closely you watch depends on the ages of your children, how independent they are, and how well they do in school. Most children need help learning to plan their time wisely, but the most important thing to remember is that it is still *their* homework!

Make sure that your children have all of the materials they'll need when they sit down to do homework: sharpened pencils, erasers, a bright, quiet work space, and a dictionary for looking up unfamiliar words. Turn off the television and the music, and take the phone off the hook. Make sure you're close by should your children have any questions.

A parent's attitude toward school and homework is crucial in helping children develop good study skills. Supporting your children in their scholastic efforts sends the important message that education comes first.

79.

Remember the Moment

A new baby in the house will create moments that you'll want to remember months or years from now. So despite the fact that you're swamped with laundry, feedings, and such, it's essential that you find the time to grab the camera or video recorder and focus on your baby.

Most baby photographs are taken when visitors are over, on a holiday, or on a trip. It's during the other moments—when nobody else is around, or in the middle of the night—that your baby will do something wonderful. To capture these moments, try leaving your camera out all of the time. This way, you won't miss a single unanticipated, spontaneous moment of your child's actions.

Organize your baby's pictures right after you get them developed. Date them and slip them into an album or photo box. Keep the less desirable pictures just as neat and organized in a separate place. If photographs are not catalogued right away, they tend to get stuffed in a drawer. Five years from now, you'll find hundreds of undated photographs. You'll then have to guess at your child's age by the clothes worn in the photo or the event that was captured.

Home movies and videos need to be catalogued and dated as soon as possible, too. Once a cassette has been filled with memories, name it according to the events it records and file it in your video library.

Photographs and home movies are something you and your spouse will enjoy for years to come. As your baby grows older, she will love looking at pictures of herself and watching home movies. Who knows? She may even prefer to watch her family's home videos over store-bought or rented ones!

80.

Parenting Rule #1:
Parents Don't Get Sick!

There is one rule that every new parent should know. Parents cannot ever get sick. Obviously, it is unavoidable at times. Your sick children insist on drooling all over you and coughing in your food. But parents must learn to be especially aware of catching germs from their sick kids, because when you do have sick kids, it takes every ounce of your strength to care for them!

When your kids are sick, there's always that urge to hug them and kiss them to make it all better. Most parents choose to throw caution to the wind by giving them the love and attention they so desperately need. After all, they're so vulnerable! How could any parents not offer comfort to children like that?

But when that thermometer rises, look for other ways to comfort your sick children—a kiss on the top of the head, a long hug, or even an offer to sit through their favorite video tapes. All can provide the comfort they crave without exposing yourself to sickness.

This is sound advice. The worst scenarios occur when a parent falls ill. When your spouse has left for work, the baby is calling out, your toddler is crying, and you're too sick to lift your head off the pillow—you have to anyway. You have to get up and function for the next ten hours until your spouse comes home and takes over. You need to prepare meals, keep the kids busy, and quite possibly pick up some milk and the dry cleaning.

It may be that your head is pounding, your throat is burning, and your body is filled with aches and pains—but you have to perform. That's something to consider the next time that you smother your feverish baby's face with kisses!

81.

You Are Not Super-Parents!

Have you ever met one of those mothers who has an immaculate home, despite having five children? Or who can offer "I-just-dropped-by" houseguests an array of freshly baked muffins and fresh fruit salad? Do you know one of those fathers who, despite running a busy corporation, still manages to play catch with his son every evening? Or a man who keeps the yard in tip-top shape on weekends in between running from soccer practice to Little League to dance class?

In a perfect world, we would all have immaculate floors, fully stocked fridges, and a lot of time to garden. We could spend entire weekends watching our children participate in sporting events and art classes, rather than running off to the hardware store, the supermarket, or the laundry. We could feed the neighborhood, should they just happen to drop by, and keep the cars spotless inside and out.

But the world isn't a perfect place. And save for a few "super-parents" who seem to do it all, it's just not realistic to believe that you can function as perfect parents all the time.

However, you can be perfect parents in other ways. You can work at prioritizing your life on a daily basis in order to leave room for the important things, such as spending quality time with your children. A better world is one where your children are always happy, well-fed, healthy, and positive. If you've managed to achieve this for your children, don't despair over the fact that your yard may be overgrown or your floors are a bit dirty. Let all that go. Happy and healthy kids are more of an achievement than any super-parents could hope for.

82.

Become an Expert
in Parenting

Wouldn't it be great if you could go to school and get a degree in parenting? Then you would know what to do when the baby won't stop crying, or when the toddler refuses to give up the bottle. You would know how to react when your third-grader gets into a fight at school or when a teenager stays out all night.

Unfortunately, there is no B.A. in mothering or B.S. in fathering. New parents are left to fend for themselves. "It will come naturally," our parents say when the baby is due and we're worried. Well, what happens when it doesn't?

In almost every community today, there are classes being offered on parenting. These classes are support groups taught by people who have been there and can now share their experiences and expertise with you. A phone call to your local hospital or family-counseling agency can provide you with a list of programs being offered. Bottle-weaning, toilet-training, power struggles—

look hard enough and you'll find a course that suits your particular parenting needs.

Parenting skills are learned by experience, but no one ever said they had to be learned by your experience. When others share their stories, you will gain information and comfort that you are not in this by yourself. Don't be afraid to register for a class and learn what others have to say—you'll find a room full of parents just like you who are still waiting for it to "come naturally." Nobody is going to think your questions or comments are ridiculous. In fact, you'll more than likely gain many solutions and suggestions for your problems.

83.

Take Your Children Out for Dinner

Here are some tips to make eating out with your kids an enjoyable experience for everyone involved. Begin with a simple phone call ahead to the restaurant of your choice. Ask if they have high chairs and room for strollers. If you're going to a full-service restaurant, ask how long it typically takes to be served once the order is taken. Cafeterias, smorgasbords, and buffets make excellent choices for family dinner excursions—and pizza is always a sure-fire hit with kids!

Before you leave the house, pack a restaurant bag with your children. Include their favorite small books, some blank paper, a coloring book, and a small package of crayons. Small, quiet items such as little cars or dolls also make excellent table toys. Don't forget to pack your children's spillproof cups and silverware from home if they need these items to manage dinner.

Don't take starving children into a restaurant and expect them to wait for the food to come. It's a good idea to offer your children a little snack (fruit, vegetables, crackers, or yogurt) on the way to the restaurant to combat any impending hunger. Hungry children are not patient children, and they will most likely become irritable and cranky if service is slow.

Talk to your children about restaurant manners. Tell them that they need to speak quietly so that they don't disturb anybody else. If possible, choose a table in a corner or against a wall so that your children have less to look at behind them. This will keep them from constantly turning around, and will keep them out of the waiter's way.

It's best to put orders for your children's meals in right away. The food should come quickly, and the kids can eat their main courses while you are ordering and dessert while you enjoy your entrée. If the restaurant does not offer a kids' menu, ask the waiter to tailor dishes for your children—the operative word here is *plain*. Ask for all garnishes on the side. Little kids are known to throw fits if any "yucky" sorts of food are touching their hamburgers.

If your children become difficult while you're waiting for your food, take them for a walk to the restroom. Visit the potty or just wash up—this can be a good distraction technique for restless children.

Insist that your children stay put during dinner. Once you give them the freedom to roam around the restaurant, you've lost control. Leave as soon as your meal is finished. Young children cannot be expected to sit still while their parents are lingering over dessert and coffee.

Above all, expect that your children will cause you some form of embarrassment—it's bound to happen when you mix kids with restaurants. Just be prepared, and you may be able to minimize it!

84.

Talk to Your Teenage Son

Most teenage boys don't interact with many adults other than their teachers and parents. Grownups are stressed, overworked, and preoccupied for the most part, and young boys are simply uninterested in having anything to do with them.

If you're looking to communicate with your teenage son, you'll have to first spend time with him doing what he likes to do and listening to what he has to say. Like it or not, you may also have to spend a little time playing video games. Some of the best parent/son conversations have taken place over a game of Super Mario Brothers.

Try listening to how your son interacts with his buddies. Discover what they enjoy doing. Are they headed over to the baseball field after school, or are they shooting hoops in the driveway? You don't have to offer to join them or hang around to the point where you make them uncomfortable, but just listening for ten minutes or so will give you a little insight as to what kind of a boy your son is. This will make it easier for the two of you to have a conversation.

Teenage boys are not as sophisticated or reliant on words as adults. Their bodies are full of energy and strength, which makes them head for the basketball court more often than the park bench for a "talk." If you really want to connect with a teenage boy, you have to get active. Challenge him to a game of one-on-one. Take him out for a round of mini-golf. This energetic atmosphere may help to break the ice and open the lines of communication.

You can also try some outrageous conversation-starters to hook your son's interest! Pick irreverent topics that will surprise and entertain him. Share a secret or two with him—the more dramatic the better. Our sons know we're not perfect, so get your mistakes out in the open, and shock him into thinking you're the most interesting human on the planet! Tell him about the time you came close to being fired, or about the time you slipped and fell in the mud just before a job interview. He'll appreciate the excitement of the story, and the sharing of secrets is bound to bring you a little closer.

Not enough parents take the time to discuss the future with their sons—not the future they hope he will aspire to, but the future he dreams of for himself. Make it your duty to ask your son about his dreams and press him to think bigger and bolder. He'll appreciate it immensely, and he'll be excited to have you take such an intense interest in his aspirations.

85.

Talk to Your Teenage Daughter

Many parents who have raised both girls and boys have observed that boys are more likely to leave the scene of a disagreement, while girls tend to make a stand and argue. One reason may be that many girls don't bottle their feelings and emotions—instead, they let it all out. Teenage girls are the worst offenders: They can often use words that are angry and hurtful.

Psychologists who have studied parent/daughter relationships say that full-scale arguments between both parties can be avoided if parents can just learn how to listen. This isn't easy.

Your daughter is mad at you for not extending her curfew. The argument has escalated into a shouting match. In order to deal with your daughter, you need to put your own emotions on hold and try to decipher what she's saying and thinking, identify the words which describe what she's feeling, and feed those words back to her in a way that asks for verification. If she tells you that you don't understand, say to her, "Okay, so please tell me what I don't understand." Before any shouting starts, ask her to talk more about it so that you can really get a chance to listen. "I can hear that you're angry. Is it the curfew, or is it something else?" You've tuned into her emotions in a way that lets her know that you're listening. If you can stop an escalating argument and say instead, "This sounds important to you. Tell me why," you'll be able to turn things around.

Try calling a "time-out" when a scene between you and your daughter becomes overly emotional. Some teens resist this idea first, but they'll ultimately appreciate the fact that they're given time to calm down. No one likes being out of control. When cooler heads prevail, she'll have had time to organize her thoughts and consider why you are against a later curfew in the first place.

One thing to look for is patterns that emerge among the circumstances that set off you and your daughter. For example, do you always find yourselves fighting after your daughter's been out with her friends? Or do you always find yourselves fighting around homework time? Maybe there is something happening within your daughter's peer group that is causing her distress. Maybe there's a problem at school. Identifying these patterns and discussing them with your daughter may help to solve her problems and avoid future flare-ups.

In the end, you and your daughter may never reach a comparable solution to your problems. If that's so, you may have to play the "because I said so" card and ask her to accept your rule anyway. Chances are that she'll be unhappy, but if you've honestly heard your daughter out, she'll at least be satisfied that you really do understand her feelings and value her point of view.

86.

A Place of Their Own

It is possible to design the perfect bedrooms for your children—ones that they will like—and keep them "in style," at least until the children enter kindergarten. But before you plunk down a lot of cash for furnishings you think they'll like, sit down with them and discuss the hopes and dreams they have for their own little places.

How much input should your child have, exactly? After all, if he's just about ready to leave the crib, he's probably old enough to have an opinion, but not old enough to know what's best for him. You should definitely take his ideas into consideration, but in the long run, compromise. You don't want to go and plaster the walls with cartoon wallpaper only to find that six months down the line, he hates those characters now.

Instead, should your child ask for character wallpaper, opt for a temporary border with that character, and he'll still have that sense of "ownership." Throw in some character sheets and curtains, and you have a system that can be replaced on a whim!

Other fun options you can use for incorporating your child into the decorating plans include stenciling the walls. Practice first on poster board, and then tape it up to see how it will look in the room. Or try sponge painting or block painting. Even toddlers can help with this process.

Selecting a bed for your child is often the most difficult part in designing the room. Back when you were expecting and you were looking for a crib, you knew what you needed: something to match the color scheme of the nursery and something that would abide by safety laws. But buying a bed presents more of a problem, especially since you don't know whether or not your child will want to sleep in it!

Many parents often make the mistake of buying a full-size bed as a first bed for a child, with the hopes of it lasting well into later years. But many children who make the move from the crib find a full-size bed too vast and scary to sleep in. If you absolutely must have a full-size bed, try starting your child on just the mattress and boxspring. Feeling closer to the floor may help your child make the adjustment. Steer clear from toddler beds such as the racing car or the dollhouse bed—your child will soon outgrow one like this, and you'll be back to square one again in no time.

87.

Give Your Kids Healthy Food

It's easy to slip into the habit of giving your children unhealthy foods to eat—especially when it becomes a matter of convenience. But by allowing your kids to eat improperly, you're creating unhealthy eating habits in your children—something that may follow them through adolescence and into adulthood.

Feeding your children healthy meals and snacks may take some extra effort, but going the extra distance to provide healthier alternatives is really worth it! Here are some common sense tips for helping our children form good eating habits:

When your child says, "I'm hungry," don't make the child wait an hour until dinner. Offer a snack of raw vegetables.

Determine the difference between a hungry child and a bored child. A hungry child will eat (fruit, veggies, cheese), while a bored child will not mention hunger once occupied by something else.

Don't give up on picky eaters. Studies indicate that children need to taste new foods several times before they acquire a taste for them.

After school is when your child is most likely to get hit by a "snack attack," and since this attack can happen quite quickly, you have to be prepared. If there are fatty chips in your house when the kids have a snack attack, that's what they're going to grab. The best thing you can do to encourage healthy eating is to keep your refrigerator stocked with easy-to-grab, health-conscious choices.

Fresh fruits such as grapes, bananas, and cantaloupes are the best sweet eats for feeding your child's hunger and boosting her energy after school. If your child refuses to eat fruit, try frozen fruit pops or yogurt pops instead.

Vegetables go perfectly with homework—carrot crunching does wonders for relieving math-induced stress! Try baby carrots, pepper slices, celery, or broccoli. Serve with dip, dressing, or salsa.

For an easy-to-grab after-school snack, try prepackaged puddings, yogurt, part-skim mozzarella sticks, or a cold glass of chocolate milk. Pair with a handful of crackers, a few breadsticks, or a low-fat muffin. Now this healthy snack can substitute for a healthy dinner. Along the same lines, low-fat cereal, granola, Chex, pretzels (hard or warm-baked soft), and peanut butter and jelly on crackers or rice cakes are better choices than chips, fried snacks, or processed cookies.

Your children are developing eating habits that will affect their weight status and what they choose to put into their bodies for the rest of their lives. With healthy eating habits at home, your kids can learn to make good food choices for the future.

88.

Take Care of
Your Sick Child

The general rule for parents with sick kids is to trust your instincts! You know your children best, and if something in your gut is telling you this is no run-of-the-mill drip, it's best to pick up the phone and call. Parents should never be worried that they're calling too much, or that their concerns are silly or stupid. When your children's health is at stake, no question is silly or stupid. Late night panic calls and early morning emergency room visits are all part of the job!

Of course, parents always need to be on top of their children's complaints and symptoms. Sometimes a bad scrape or an upset tummy can be worse than it appears. If your child's symptoms get worse or seem unusual, call the doctor's office immediately—especially if he's vomiting or has diarrhea that lasts for more than a few hours. Always investigate a rash of any kind (particularly when accompanied by a fever) and a cough or cold that does not get better in several days.

Where minor illness is concerned, making your children feel better should be your primary concern. Create a "sick child station" in your living room, complete with fluffy pillows, warm blankets and your children's favorite comfort toys. Settle the sick one on the sofa, as cozy as possible. Let him watch as much television or as many videos as he wants—when discomfort strikes, kids need the mindless distraction television offers.

Trust the soup! For ages, Jewish grandmothers have pushed chicken soup on their sick patients, and for good reason! The salty, warm liquid is perfect for soothing a sore throat, the chicken is full of protein, and the noodles are nourishing and won't further upset queasy tummies.

Hydrate, hydrate, hydrate, especially with a fever. Children lose body water quickly when they are sick, and it needs to be replenished or they may dehydrate. Keep a water bottle close by, and try to get him to drink.

Most importantly, sit with your child, even if he keeps dozing off. If you have bills to do or calls to make, set yourself up next to him on the sofa and work from there. It will bring him great comfort to have you next to him and to see your face each time he wakes up.

89.

Discipline the Positive Way

Discipline is the way we guide and teach our children about acceptable behavior within certain limits. Discipline is not the same as punishment, which implies that a child is wrong, and deals with the past. Discipline treats the behavior as something negative, and deals with the present and the future.

Knowing right from wrong is a concept that takes time and experience to understand. Young children need adults to watch them and protect them from harm because they can't be expected to remember all of the rules and limitations set for them. It is normal for young children to misbehave because they are just learning the rules.

In order to teach your kids right from wrong, you know that you'll have to discipline them. You also know that you need to give yourself time to deal with your anger over your children's misbehavior. If your five-year-old has flooded the bathroom, your first instinct may be to give the child a swat on the behind. But then you haven't taught him anything. Take a moment and deal with your anger over the mess before taking it out on him. Turn off the faucet, take a few deep breaths, go alone into another room and scream if you have to, and then find your son and deal with him in a calmer manner. Give him a time-out. Take away a privilege. Have him help with the cleanup. But explain to him why you are angry and why he mustn't do something like that again. Now perhaps he'll understand why he shouldn't flood the bathroom.

Disciplining kids isn't easy. Physical punishment such as spanking, hitting, slapping, or shaking should never be used. It may cause children to act out of fear rather than motivation to strive for responsible behavior. Children who are physically punished may develop low self-esteem and be aggressive. Hitting your children doesn't teach them anything except hitting. Taking away a privilege shows your child that you are serious about changing his behavior and causes him to think and learn from the experience.

Try using humor when disciplining your children. It can reduce tension or help to defuse a power struggle. Plus it can encourage both you and your children not to take your problems so seriously. Don't overuse humor, however. You don't want to give your children the idea that they're being charming when they're doing something harmful.

When you need help disciplining your children, ask a professional! Children typically grow and learn new skills at their own paces. Sometimes they may need a bit of extra help to stay on track. And sometimes the parents are the ones in need of help as they struggle to sort out the best approaches to parenting.

90.

Finishing a Sentence

As any parent with children older than two knows, finishing a sentence is hands-down the most difficult thing to achieve during the course of any given day. Even if you're a normal parent and you have normal children, you have no doubt lived through countless interrupted conversations and a multitude of unfinished sentences.

How do you get your kids to stop interrupting you? First, you must teach your children that interrupting others is just plain poor manners. This may confuse your children, especially if they've interrupted you by saying, "Excuse me!" If your children remember to interrupt you with "excuse me," first praise them, then reprimand them for interrupting.

Many parents admonish their children for interrupting, but in the same breath they respond to the children's interrupted requests! That doesn't fly with persistent young children. Once they figure out that they'll get you to answer their requests despite the fact that you're speaking with somebody else, their behavior will continue.

Wanting another cookie does not warrant an interruption. Interrupting a parent's phone call to say that the house is on fire does. Your children can learn the difference between something that needs immediate attention and something that doesn't. Instruct your children to wait for a pause in your conversation (provided there's no emergency) and say, "Excuse me." When they do, be sure to respond positively. For example, if a request is something that can wait until you're finished, you can say, "Sweetheart, I heard you ask me for another cookie, but please wait until I finish talking, and we can discuss it." Then continue your conversation.

Another good way to teach your children to curb their interruptions is to prepare a special, quiet sign between you that lets you know they need you and lets them know that you understand. Perhaps they could gently squeeze your hand if they need to ask you a question while you're speaking to someone else. Then you can squeeze back to indicate that you'll be with your child in just a moment. The worst thing that you can do is engage your children in a discussion about interrupting—while they're interrupting! "You're interrupting me! And no, you cannot have a cookie, it's almost time for dinner!" Instead, look them in the eye, say, "I'll listen to you in just a minute," and return to your conversation. Stick to this method, and never give in to tantrums. Your kids will soon learn that you're not going to respond when they interrupt, and eventually they'll develop the patience to wait until you're through talking.

91.

Get Your Kids to Cooperate

The most frequent complaint of parents today is, "My children don't do what I tell them to do." Mainly, it's because there are so many things that parents want their kids to do that they become quickly exasperated just by having to ask so much. It's not as if you can afford to wait for your children to start cooperating on their own—that's not going to happen. But with the use of consistent, effective parenting skills, you can learn to change your children's behavior and encourage them to cooperate willingly on a regular basis.

First of all, be clear and specific about what you want done. Making general comments such as, "This basement is a mess!" when you want your kids to clean the basement isn't going to work. Instead, tell them specifically, "Kids, I want you to clean the basement right now!" It's also important to avoid beginning requests with, "Will you?" "Could you?" or "Would you?" This sends your children the message that honoring your request is optional.

It's also essential to stay clear of distractions when asking your children to do something. You can waste plenty of time (not to mention breath!) telling an eight-year-old to get ready for school if the child is sitting in the vicinity of a television that's on. Shut off the television first. Waiting for a commercial is a good idea—if you're not in a rush—in order to avoid putting the child on the defensive.

Give your children results that motivate them to perform tasks: "Once you've cleaned the basement, you can go outside to play." When they're given something to work for (do not confuse this with bribery!), your children are more apt to complete the task that has been asked of them.

As often is the case with children, the more choices you offer them, the more in control of the situation they'll feel. If you're tired of asking your children to do something, give them an option: "Which would you like to do first, pick up your clothes or put away your toys?" By giving your children a choice, they'll learn to live with the consequences of their decisions and feel as if they are being given more control of the situation.

Most importantly, try to keep your emotions from taking over. Many parents often resort to yelling and threatening their children when they've become fed up with noncompliance. Remember, in your kids' minds, you're interrupting their activities with tasks that you want completed and that they don't want to do. Before resorting to yelling and screaming, give your kids just a little more time to motivate themselves. They may surprise you by responding exactly the way you'd hoped—it may be an hour later than you would have liked, but at least it will get done!

92.

Monitor "the Box"

merican children watch an average of three to four hours of television a day. When you consider that television can be a powerful influence in developing values and shaping behavior, it's a good idea to look at what your kids are watching on TV.

Research has shown that the effects of television violence on children and teens can cause them to become immune to the horror of violence, or to accept violence as a way to solve problems. Children learn to imitate the violence that they see on TV, and when they see shows in which the violence is very realistic, is frequently repeated, and goes unpunished, they are even more likely to imitate it. Violence on television isn't the only source for violent behavior in children, but it is a significant contributor.

Monitor what your children are watching on television. Never trust that a television show is going to be appropriate for your children just because it is on a "kids' network"—or because friends of yours let their children watch. Screen all programs before letting your kids tune in to anything.

Set limits on the amount of time your children spend watching TV. Some parents only let their kids watch one hour a day, in the evening, after all homework has been completed. Others limit their children's viewing to just mornings, before school. Determine which viewing times are best for your children and how much time is appropriate, and be sure to sit with them and see what they watch.

For young children who witness violence on TV, it's important to teach them the difference between television and reality. Point out that actors are not actually hurt or killed, and that similar violence in real life results in pain or death. Flat-out refuse to let your children watch programs known to be violent, and change the channel if something offensive comes on while they're in the room with you. Be sure to disapprove of violent episodes in front of your children, and stress the belief that such behavior is not a good way to resolve problems.

Sometimes your children will beg you to let them watch a show because "everyone at school watches." If this is the case in your house, it's a good idea to contact other parents and discuss the situation with them. You may come to an agreement to enforce similar rules about outlawing certain programs.

Ultimately, the amount of time children watch television should be moderated, regardless of content. TV keeps them from participating in other activities such as reading, playing with friends, and participating in more physical activities.

93.

Oh, Fiddlesticks!

Quick—what do you do when your children use profanity? If your answer is, "Wash their mouths out with soap," you're not right, but it's the same answer that many other parents gave in a recent magazine poll about discipline! Perhaps that approach worked in the past, but it also reinforces negative behavior by using negative behavior. For an adult to wash a child's mouth out with soap, the child must first be restrained, and then the soap must be stuck forcibly in the mouth. This constitutes a fairly violent act. Not only is it abusive, but it violates the parent-child trust.

No matter what we do to keep our children from hearing profanity, they will eventually hear that language from other kids. At school, in camp, or on the bus, our children are going to hear many words—sometimes at a very young age—that we don't want them to hear. And chances are that they're going to use these exciting, new words in front of us—maybe even *to* us.

Remember that as a parent, you are your child's role model, and it is your responsibility to set the standard. If you hear your child using bad language, remain calm. Explain that the word or words are not acceptable, and that they can hurt people's feelings with such words; just as hitting or kicking can hurt people, words, too, can leave bruises. Your child will need to know that other people will use profanity whether you want them to or not. Stress that your family does not believe in using bad language.

Preschoolers who swear are only imitating the language they hear around the house, so it's essential that both parents watch what they say at all times. Many times, we don't realize that we use profanity in front of our children, and if that's the case in your house, you need to avoid it. Children hear *everything*. Even if you mutter foul language under your breath or whisper it over the phone, they will still hear it. They're more apt to repeat you if you go to extremes to hide it from them. If you or your spouse has a problem curbing your use of bad language, you need to work together on ways to stop.

Finally, the most important thing you can do as a parent is to praise your child for doing or saying the right thing! If bad language has become a problem and your child catches and corrects herself before saying a bad word, be sure to tell her how proud you are of her. As with every aspect of parenting, positive reinforcement is the way to bring out the good behavior—and get rid of the bad.

94.

Home Alone

Many parents struggle with the decision of whether or not they can leave their teenage kids home alone. There is no magic age when kids suddenly develop the maturity and good sense needed to stay by themselves. However, there are recommended guidelines to help parents determine whether or not their kids are ready to stay home alone.

Young teens are physically ready to stay home by themselves (or come home from school to an empty house) when they can lock and unlock doors and windows. You need to be sure that your kids can recognize potentially dangerous situations and know how to keep themselves safe. It's also a good idea to consider how equipped they are to communicate with you if a serious problem arises.

Before you agree to let your young teenager stay home alone, even if she seems mature enough to handle it, take a few additional points into consideration. For example, timing should be a major factor when making this decision. If your family is going through a transition period due to divorce, death, remarriage, or a move, then it's probably not the best time to begin leaving her alone. In addition, you need to take into account your neighborhood and your house: Are they both safe? You should make sure there is a responsible adult nearby to whom your child can turn for help. Finally, make sure she has all of the phone numbers for everywhere that you'll be while she's home alone.

95.

What Are We Training For?

Back a few years ago, the majority of children did not go to preschool. Mothers didn't work, and they had all the time in the world to potty-train the kids. Now, with the rapidly growing number of three- and four-year-olds attending preschool, many preschools insist that children are out of diapers before they can begin attending. This presents a problem for working parents who haven't been successful potty-training their children, yet who rely on preschool and daycare programs as their main source of child care.

By using a developmental approach to potty-training, most children become ready between 24 and 36 months of age. There are three factors to consider: First, they must be physically ready. They need to be able to interpret the physical sensations telling them that they need to go and be able to "hold it in" or "let it go" at will. Second, they must have a cognitive understanding that what they need to do needs to be done in the toilet. Third, they must be emotionally ready. Children should feel that they are making the decision about when to use the toilet.

Teach your children about their bodies and how they work—this may help your children take the initiative in learning to train. When you change your children's diapers, include them in the cleaning. This will help prepare them for when they'll be doing it themselves. Many experts suggest taking training toddlers outdoors in your yard on a warm day and leaving them naked as they play. This helps them learn how their bodies work and gets them to recognize the feeling that comes just before they go to the bathroom. Always give your children clear, honest information about all of their body parts, including genitals, and teach them to come to you with any questions.

When you think they're ready, begin toilet training at home, where your child's schedule and activities are more predictable. Ultimately, you want the act of going to the bathroom to become familiar and automatic. Facilitate your children's use of the toilet by providing a step stool, flushable wipes, and a soft, cushiony toilet seat. Most importantly, be sure that your children's clothes are easy to remove and put back on, in order to avoid accidents.

It is important that children are never forced, shamed, or manipulated into using the toilet. It is your job as a parent to be ready with praise when your little ones succeed in the bathroom. And if they don't—or if they do, but then don't again—don't despair! Given time and encouragement, we all figure out how to do it on our own. Your child will, too!

96.

Reconnect with Your
Former Non-Parent Self

Do you ever find yourself wishing that you could sleep late or spend the entire day doing whatever you please, as long as it doesn't involve running an errand or carpooling your kids? Do you often dream about a weekend full of uninterrupted conversation with your spouse? Do you find yourself reflecting on the nights you spent out with your best friends when you didn't have to worry about what time you had to be up in the morning?

If you answered an enthusiastic yes to one or more of these questions, it's time you found a baby-sitter or enlisted your parents, in-laws, neighbors, or friends—and turned those dreams into reality. If you know that your kids will be well-cared for while you're away, treat yourself to a relaxing mini-vacation, and remind yourself what it was like before your world was turned upside-down with kids.

Though most people feel more comfortable planning a weekend away from their kids long in advance, you're actually better off if you can pull it off spontaneously. The reason is that once you pick a night or weekend and log it onto your family calendar, something may go wrong. Perhaps it will be a sick child, a mandatory family function, or your spouse's office party. Something may spoil your plans and result in your having to reschedule. Remember back when you weren't a parent? You never had to plan for a weekend away so far in advance. A spontaneous weekend away—an idea sparked on Thursday night and pulled together by Friday afternoon—will make it so much more exciting!

These days, spontaneous travel is even easier with the Internet right at your fingertips. You can log onto a web site that offers inexpensive airfares or reasonably priced hotel rooms and book a great place with barely any notice. Or you don't have to go far away at all—instead, head for the nearest deluxe hotel in your area and pamper yourselves with a weekend "not-away"! Many hotels offer weekend packages that include spa services, breakfast in bed, and nightly entertainment so that you can enjoy some refreshing time away—just a few short miles from home.

You owe it to yourself—and to your children—to rejuvenate your souls and reconnect with your former non-parent selves. Relive the days you spent shopping, or golfing, or dancing until the wee hours of the morning. Or just stay in bed all day and order room service. Either way, you'll come away feeling relaxed, refreshed, and rejuvenated. Plus it'll give you a chance to miss those amazing kids of yours!

97.

There Goes the
Neighborhood

Whatever your reasons for moving, the impact on your family can be considerable. That's why it's important for parents to take the time to help their kids come to terms with the changes that are happening in their family. Leaving behind people you love can be the hardest thing in the world. It's essential that parents acknowledge their children's feelings and give them the opportunity to do whatever it is they need to say good-bye.

A great idea for parents to help ease the sadness their kids may feel because of an impending move is to assure your children that they're not losing their old friends. Try to make plans for your kids to keep in touch with their friends as much as possible. Help them make change-of-address cards to hand out with e-mail addresses and telephone numbers. Plan to have their friends to come for special visits to the new house soon after the move.

Parents can help their kids adjust to a move by sharing as much information as possible. Tell them when the move is going to take place and what their new neighborhood is going to be like. If possible, visit your new home and look for an opportunity to meet your new neighbors. If you're moving across the country, take along a video camera when you visit the new place and record your home and neighborhood to share with your kids.

Keep the mood upbeat before a move. Treat the experience as an adventure. Don't focus on what you're leaving behind. Instead, talk about all the new and exciting things that you'll be able to do in your new neighborhood. Talk about the new school, the great pizza place in your new neighborhood, or the community pool and playground. Anything that will get your children excited about the move will make the transition easier.

Most importantly, involve your kids in the move! Let them choose what colors to paint their new bedrooms in the new house, and allow them to help arrange their bedroom furniture. Before you move, enlist them as packers: Give them easy jobs such as numbering or sticking identifying stickers on boxes.

Make sure not to minimize the impact that your move will have on your children, and take the time to come to terms with the changes that are happening in your family. Kids need to feel like they have some control over their lives—especially at a time when things are about to change.

98.

Kick the Whine Habit

The whining years are a phase your child will probably pass through when you'll long for the days when your child was too young to speak! There are many reasons children whine. For some children, whining is a way to get things. For others, it's a cry for help and a need for attention. Still others whine because their friends whine. There are ways to get your child to stop whining. As always, be consistent in your behavior and understand that all children whine at some time or another.

An effective way to stop your child from whining is to pretend that you don't hear anything he says when it is said in a whining voice. For example, if your son whines that he wants to go to a friend's house, reply by saying, "Is somebody talking? I hear noise, but I don't hear any normal words."

When your child is whining, bring him into a quiet room and ask him to listen to how he sounds. Point out the inflections of his whine, and then ask him to repeat the question in his "regular voice." This is effective—and often funny—for a child, who may not realize that he's whining in the first place.

Many experts believe that whining occurs when children feel powerless. If you make it a point to give them a little extra control, you may help to curb the whines that usually occur during the course of the day. If your child always whines at a sibling's sports practice, tell the child "I know you get bored, but if you don't whine this time, I'll let you choose the restaurant for dinner this evening."

In addition to "no hitting" and "no teasing," make "no whining" one of your family rules. Kids will understand what is expected of them (and what's not) right from the start.

99.

Don't Bribe Them—
Reward Them

When parents talk to other parents about bribery, they often don't mean "bribery" at all. It's all a matter of linguistics. We've always used the word "bribe" when talking about what we do to get our children to do something. But in fact, the word we should be using is "reward."

Bribery refers to coercing someone into doing something that is wrong. You should never bribe a child to do something that is wrong, illegal, or inappropriate for his age. Bribery such as this has no place in parenting.

Rewards, on the other hand, are used to entice children to behave appropriately. Rewards can be planned or spontaneous, social or tangible. Parents can use rewards to teach and reinforce good behavior. If your child behaves exceptionally well in a potentially boring or difficult situation, praise her. Tell her how much you appreciate such good behavior. By telling her this or offering hugs and kisses, you're giving a positive social reward and helping to reinforce the good behavior.

If your child is in the habit of running amok every time you need her to behave, you might decide to develop a reward system: "I'll give you a nickel if you play nicely with the toys while I get my haircut." That's a tangible reward—something you can offer for several weeks in a row, with the intention of changing the child's negative behavior pattern into a positive one. After several weeks, if she is still misbehaving at the salon, you'll know your reward system failed, and you must look for another method.

Be wary of overusing the reward method—especially if you find yourself giving your children a tangible reward every time that they behave as expected. When this happens, the tables have turned in the relationship. You have, perhaps without realizing it, developed the threat or fear that if you don't provide a prize, your child will misbehave intentionally. It's time to drop the treat connected to the good behavior.

Children need to learn how to behave without being dependent on a treat. If you let them know what to expect and then give them positive feedback for their good behavior, you'll have a great system that will work wonders!

100.

Focus on the Future

Parents dream about their children's future. You hope your children will grow to be happy, healthy, and successful individuals. You look forward to when they graduate from college, get married, and have children of their own. Everyone wants the best for their children—which is why it's a good idea to begin preparing for your family's future now.

Before you know it, your first baby will be three months old. Then twelve months. Then the baby is suddenly three, and you have another. Raising a family can be one of life's richest and most rewarding experiences, as well as one of the most challenging things you'll ever do in life, and yet, no matter how you live, it all just goes by so quickly. Creating balance in life to spend quality time with your family should be your biggest priority.

Consider your family a work in progress as you head into the future. It is always growing, always learning. Of course, one of your top priorities is to prepare for your family's future financially. That said, make sure you invest wisely and always with the best intentions of your family at heart. Start saving for your children's college fund the moment that they're born, and when they're older and understand the value of money, encourage them to save, save, save.

But you can't build for your family's future with money alone. Money is certainly important—but it's not the most important thing. Happiness, good health, compassion, love, and knowledge are some of the keys to helping your family grow. Understand that you can't head toward the future without focusing on your family's past and present. Who you are and what you were will help shape the family you're going to become.

Document everything along the way. Create a family scrapbook, and fill it with photos, birth announcements, report cards, family portraits, locks of hair—any little pieces of family history that you want recorded. Keep these scrapbooks in fireproof boxes to make sure that they'll be safe forever. Research your family's history together with your children—online or through your library—and explain to them who each person was and what their link is to that person.

Read to your children—and read to them often! Encourage them to explore their imaginations by writing their own storybooks.

Get down on the floor and play games with your kids. Ignore your aching back or your trick knees and just play!

Try not to miss their soccer games, dance recitals, or class trips.

Send your children notes in their lunchboxes, or leave them notes on their pillows at night. And don't stop—even when they're in high school.

You can never go back. Before you know it, they'll be leaving the house, and you'll find yourself longing for those hectic days when they were little and they filled the rooms with noise and laughter on the weekends. All you have is the present, so make the best of it by not shortchanging your children. Spend as much time with them as possible, and together you can prepare for the lifetime of love and family experiences that lie ahead.